HIGHER

Geography

course notes

Text copyright © 2004 Dr Bill Dick
Design and layout copyright © 2004 Leckie & Leckie Ltd
Cover image © Getty Images

1st edition (reprinted 2006, 2007)

For Christine, Duncan and Louisa

Published by
Leckie & Leckie Ltd, 3rd Floor, 4 Queen Street, Edinburgh, EH2 1JE
tel: 0131 220 6831 fax: 0131 225 9987
enquiries@leckieandleckie.co.uk www.leckieandleckie.co.uk

Special thanks to
Caleb Rutherford (design), Hamish Sanderson (illustration),
Rob Hands (proofreading)

ISBN-13 978-184372-080-5
ISBN 1-84372-080-9

A CIP Catalogue record for this book is available from the British Library.

® Leckie & Leckie is a registered trademark.

Leckie & Leckie is a division of Huveaux plc.

Leckie & Leckie would like to thank the following organisations for their kind permission to reproduce their material:
Scottish Qualifications Authority for use of Past Paper questions;
Ordnance Survey mapping on behalf of the controller of Her Majesty's Stationery Office© for the reproduction of O.S. Maps on pages 67, 69, 132, 133, 164.

✕ Dr Bill Dick ✕

CONTENTS

Section 2 – The Human Environment (Paper 1)

Section 3 – Environmental Interactions (Paper 2)

INTRODUCTION & EXAM ADVICE

INTRODUCTION

The aim of this revision guide is to provide a handbook which, when used in conjunction with your class notes and textbooks, will help you to maximise the number of marks you can obtain in the national examinations in Higher Grade Geography.

All of the text is written from an examination point of view. Consequently, this guide is not intended to replace your course books but rather to supplement them for revision purposes. There are certain key elements that examiners look for in responses to questions set. It follows that there are certain basic areas of the course material that candidates must know and which should be included in answers. Helping you to become aware of what is necessary and what is not essential in preparing for the exams is the guiding principle of these notes.

Text sections

In these sections there are key points which have been designed to act as guides for you to study elements of the syllabus. Some of these key points are illustrated with maps, diagrams and reference data, most of which have been taken from past question papers. The text accompanying these points provides a basis for your answers. Whichever topics you study in the Environmental Interactions section, they should be studied together with the relevant core topic, for example, Urban / Urban Change and Management, Lithosphere / Rural Land Resources.

Higher Syllabus

In 2003 the Higher grade Arrangements and Syllabus were subject to review by SQA.
In the new syllabus arrangements, what had previously been the Core and Applications sections are now described as the Physical Environment, the Human Environment (Paper I) and Environmental Interactions (Paper II).
The syllabus has also changed to include certain additional topics such as 'coasts' within the Lithosphere section and the Rural Land Resources Environmental Interactions section. A number of topics have been deleted from other parts of the syllabus, for example, 'scarp and vale landscapes', and 'derelict and abandoned land' have been removed from the Lithosphere and Biosphere core topics to compensate for the new additions.
These changes have been incorporated into this book.

The examination

There will also be a number of changes to the structure of the actual examination in terms of the number of topics examined in both papers, the marks totals for questions and papers and the length of the papers. These changes have been noted in this text.

Paper I will consist of three Sections.

Section A will have 4 compulsory questions from the 4 physical environment and 4 human environment topics.

Section B will have 2 physical questions asking you to answer 1 of these.

Section C will have 2 Human questions asking you to answer 1 of these.

The marks total for Paper I is 50 marks.

Paper II will ask you to answer 2 questions from a choice of 6.

The marks total for Paper II is 50 marks.

Since the textbook was first published, the Scottish Qualifications Authority have amended the Arrangements for the examination to the effect that the total number of marks for both papers will be doubled in the 2008 examination. The total marks available for paper 1 will be 100 and that for paper 2 will be 100 giving a total of 200 marks for the whole exam. This effectively dispenses with the use of 1/2 marks. When reading the sections of the text dealing with sample questions, answers and marking instructions simply double the marks shown. Thus the total marks gained for the following answer, for example, would change from 4 1/2 marks out of 6 to 9 marks out of 12.

EXAMINATION ADVICE

- When revising you can use this guide together with past examination questions and revise topic by topic, e.g. Urban – settlement zones or Population – migration factors.

- If you are asked for a named country or city, make sure you include details of any case study you have covered. Avoid vague answers when asked for detail. Avoid vague terms such as *'dry soils'* or *'fertile soils'* if you can give more detailed information, e.g. *'deep and well drained soils'* or *'rich in nutrients'*.

- Read the instructions carefully. If asked to describe and explain make sure that you refer to both in your answer.

- If you are given data in the form of maps, diagrams and tables in the question, make sure you use this information in your answer to support any points of view you give. If describing climates, give climate figures.

- Be guided by the number of marks for a question as to the length of your answer.

- Watch your time and do not spend too much time on any particular answer thus leaving yourself short of time to finish the paper. Try to time yourself during the examination for each question. Make sure that you leave yourself sufficient time to answer all of the questions.

- If there is a certain amount of predictability in the topics being asked each year, go through past papers to review topics previously asked and this might help you to prioritise your study topics.

- If you have any time left in the exam, use it to go back over your answers to see if you can add anything to what you have written by way of additional text including more examples or diagrams which you may have omitted.

- Use the selected sample question and answer sections to revise. Attempt the questions and check your answers against the marking instructions which are included at the end of the sample questions. Remember, if you mark your answers, award a half mark for every correct statement or appropriate example.

- You may wish to use the mind mapping technique to help you revise individual topics. Examples of these are included within the text.

- For the actual examination, prepare your notes into sections. Try to work out a schedule for studying with a programme which includes which sections of the syllabus you intend to study.

- Check your knowledge of the topics from time to time using past paper questions.

- Organise your notes into checklists and revision cards.

- Try to avoid leaving your studying to a day or two before the exam. Also try to avoid cramming your studies on the night before the examination, especially staying up late to study.

- Practice drawing diagrams which may be included in your answers for example, corries or pydramidal peaks.

- Make sure you know the examination timetable, noting the dates and times of your examinations. Give yourself plenty of time by arriving early for the examination, well equipped with pens, pencils, rubbers etc.

- If you have any time left at the end, use this time productively by going back over your answers and perhaps adding additional parts to your answer. This is especially helpful in Ordnance Survey based questions.

- Make sure that you have read the instructions on the question carefully and that you have avoided needless errors such as answering the wrong sections or failing to *explain* when asked to or perhaps omitting to refer to a named area or case study.

- One technique, which you might find helpful, especially when answering long questions worth 10 or more marks, is to 'brain storm' for possible points for your answer. You can write these down in a list at the start of your answer. As you go through your answer you can double check with your list to ensure that you have put as much detail into your answer as you can. It avoids coming out of the exam and being annoyed that you forgot to mention an important point.

The Physical Environment

1 – Atmosphere

2 – Hydrosphere

3 – Lithosphere

4 – Biosphere

ATMOSPHERE

The study of atmosphere forms the first part of the physical environment element of the Higher Geography course. This involves an understanding of a wide range of concepts and theories relating to variations in world temperature and rainfall patterns and their effects. For the purposes of the examination, this can be reduced to the study of a specific number of aspects of atmosphere and climate.

The first of these involves the understanding of how the earth receives energy in the form of heat, how that energy is distributed and redistributed both within the earth and back to space and how this pattern creates a system of movement of air around the earth.

GLOBAL SCALE

Key Point 1

You should be able to explain, using an appropriate diagram, why tropical latitudes receive more solar energy than polar regions

The amount of heat or energy received by the Earth from the sun varies throughout different parts of the earth. This is due mainly to the effect of *latitude*. This is shown in Figure 1·1.

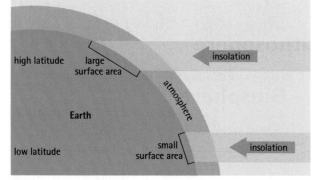

Figure 1·1 – *Variation in earth's insolation*

Effect of latitude on distribution of solar energy:

1. Places at the equator or between the tropics are always hotter than places at higher latitudes. This is because the earth is a sphere and the sun's rays strike the areas around the centre of the earth at right angles.
2. At higher latitudes the rays strike the surface at a wider angle. The net effect of this is that surfaces nearer the equator receive more insolation, i.e. sun's heat, than surfaces nearer the poles.
3. The insolation striking the surface at the equator heats up a smaller surface area than the same amount of insolation at higher latitudes.

Key Point 2

You should be able to explain why there is a net gain of solar energy in the Tropical latitudes and a net loss towards the Poles

This is due to Earth's movement around the sun.
* The earth revolves around the sun. However, the Earth is tilted from the perpendicular by 23.5°. Therefore the sun is directly overhead at the equator and each of the tropics at different times of the year.
* When the sun apparently appears directly overhead the equator these times are called the *maxima* and are also termed the *equinoxes*.
* When the sun is directly over the tropics, this is termed the *solstices*. During the winter solstice in the northern hemisphere, the amount of insolation received at the North Pole is zero.
* At the poles there are alternately six months of light and six months of darkness.

Key Point 3

You should be able to describe the distribution of the amount of solar energy which is absorbed by the earth. This is known as the earth's heat budget

* Figure 1·2 shows a summary of the energy which the earth receives from the sun and how it is distributed.
* The earth is heated by energy in the form of solar rays from the sun. Some of this energy is absorbed directly by land and water, some is interrupted by clouds and dust in the atmosphere and some is reflected back into space before even reaching the earth's surface.
* For every 100 units of energy which the earth receives, 31 units are reflected back into space [*from clouds (17), gases and dust (8) and from the earth's surface (6)*].
* This reflected energy is called the earth's albedo.
* A further 23 units are absorbed by clouds, water vapour, dust and various gases.
* The remaining 46 units are absorbed by the earth's surface land and water.

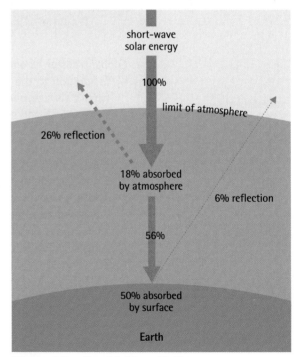

Figure 1·2 – Earth's Heat Budget

Key Point 4

You should be able to describe the factors which affect the amount of sunlight reflected from the earth's surface

The most important points to note include:
- Energy absorbed by the earth causes the earth's temperature to rise. Energy (in the form of long-wave radiation) radiates back from the surface into the atmosphere where it is absorbed by clouds and gases. These clouds and gases are heated and they in turn radiate energy, some of which is returned to the earth's surface.
- The return of this energy from the atmosphere once again heats the surface and helps to maintain surface temperatures.
- Energy which would be reflected back into space is trapped and reflected back to the surface by the clouds and gases; this causes the atmosphere to heat up further creating what is called the '**greenhouse effect**'.
- Most of the energy which heats the atmosphere actually comes from the earth's surface.
- This happens through conduction, that is energy rising from the earth's surface and through latent heat given out when evaporated water rises from the surface and condenses in the atmosphere releasing heat as it does so.

Key Point 5

You must be able to describe the role of atmospheric circulation in the redistribution of energy over the globe. This is called 'Global Transfer of Energy'

Global transfer of energy is due to the following:
- In addition to the vertical transfer of energy between the atmosphere and the earth's surface, energy is also transferred between the equator and the poles.
- Areas north and south of latitude 38°, receive less solar energy than areas between latitudes 38°N and 38°S.
- In the higher latitudes more energy is emitted from the surface than absorbed. Nearer the tropics more energy is absorbed by than emitted from the surface.
- Consequently there is a deficit in solar energy north and south of latitudes 38°.
- There is also a surplus of solar energy in areas between 38°N and 38°S.
- If this situation remained static, areas near the tropics would become hotter whilst those further north and south would become colder. This does not happen is due to the transfer of energy from areas of surplus to areas of deficit.
- This transfer of energy is known as atmospheric circulation.

Key Point 6

You should be able to describe and explain how this happens using an appropriate diagram

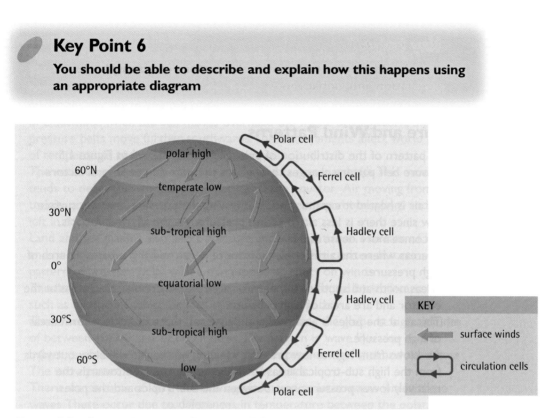

Figure 1·3 – Atmospheric circulation model

Atmospheric circulation happens because:

- At the equator the solar energy at the surface of the earth heats the air immediately above it. This air expands, becomes less dense and rises to a higher altitude creating a zone of low pressure. At the higher altitude the temperature is lower and therefore the air cools, becomes more dense and begins to fall. Pressure differences between the surface and upper atmosphere creates a wind.

- Due to the rotation of the earth and the giving out of latent heat, the cooler more dense air flows both northwards and southwards and, as it becomes even cooler and more dense, it falls as an area of high pressure. This falling air creates a high pressure zone around 30°N and 30°S. This circulation of air forms cells both north and south of the equator called *Hadley cells.*

- In addition to the Hadley cells above the tropics, cells exist above each of the poles due to cold air in these areas becoming dense and falling to create zones of high pressure. These are termed *Polar cells.*

- Some of this air moves from the high pressure area towards lower latitudes, again due to the rotation of the earth. In these lower latitudes the air is heated and begins to rise to higher altitudes where it is cooled, creating a zone of low pressure. Thus a circulation pattern of air occurs at the poles similar to that above the tropics. These are called Polar cells.

- A third cell, termed a *Ferrel cell*, forms due to the temperature differences between the first two cells at the tropics and at the poles. Warm air from the Hadley cell at the tropics feeds into the higher latitudes whilst colder air from the polar cell feeds into the lower latitudes.

- This leads to the transfer of energy from the warmer lower latitudes to the higher colder altitudes and transfer of colder air from the colder higher latitudes to the warmer lower latitudes.

> ### Key Point 10
>
> **You should be able to describe the general pattern of ocean currents on a world map**

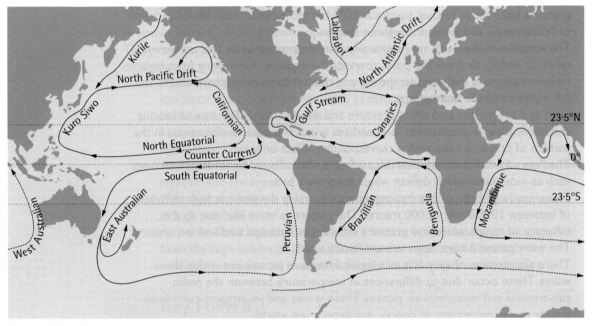

Figure 1·5 – Pattern of world's ocean currents

71% of the earth's surface is covered by water and 29% of the surface is land. This has an important influence on the transfer of energy since water is a much more efficient store of heat than land. The oceans warm more slowly than land but are heated to a greater depth. Heat is redistributed due to the flow of ocean currents. Because the waters nearer the equator receive more heat than those near the poles, warm water flows outwards from the equatorial regions towards higher latitudes. In turn, colder water from the poles flows towards warmer regions creating a circulatory system. The flow is disrupted and distorted by the effect of the earth's rotation and the distribution pattern of the world's land masses thus creating the pattern of ocean currents which exist at present.

Key Point 11

You should be able to explain this pattern

Reasons include:
- The pattern of the world's ocean currents is closely linked with the distribution of the world's main pressure belts and wind patterns.
- The land masses disrupt the flow of the currents, otherwise the pattern would be fairly straightforward. Basically in both hemispheres there would be three groups of currents, equatorial, sub-tropical and sub-arctic/antarctic. The presence of continental land masses distorts the flow of the currents producing the pattern shown in Figure 1·5.
- Winds blowing over these currents assist in the flow of warm water to cooler areas and cooler water to warmer areas.
- Due to the earth's rotation, winds in the northern hemisphere are deflected to the right and in the southern hemisphere to the left, helping to create the pattern of currents shown in Figure 1·5.
- The nature of the current (whether it is warm or cold) and the type of wind (whether it is onshore or offshore) has a vital effect on climatic conditions on the land masses.
- The pattern of ocean currents has a great influence on the temperature patterns throughout the world over the different seasons. The ocean currents are an important part of the system of circulation and transfer of energy throughout the world.

Key Point 12

You should be able to describe variations in global temperatures for the last 100 years as shown on a graph

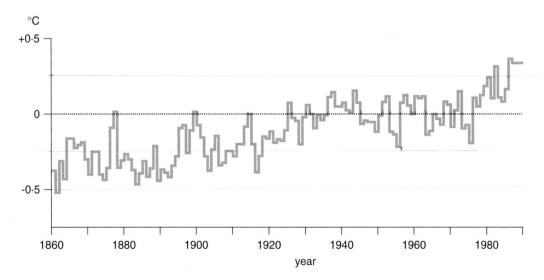

Figure 1·6 – Temperature variations from 1860 to 1990

When describing the variations on this graph you should refer to the following:
- The general trend throughout the period, mentioning whether the temperature is generally rising or falling.
- Note any minor fluctuations within the graph and when they occur. Describe the highest and lowest points on the graph and the overall range in temperature change.
- State the periods when temperatures were below and above the stated norm (for instance, in 1960). Note any times when the temperature remained fairly constant.
- Describe any periods when there were dramatic changes in the temperature.
- Refer to actual figures from the graph to illustrate your points.

Key Point 13

You should be able to suggest both physical and human reasons for variations in global temperatures for the last 100 – 150 years

Physical reasons:
- Changes in the amount of solar energy given out by the sun over time.
- Activities on the earth including volcanic eruptions and variations in the amount of atmospheric gases present which may have changed the amount of solar radiation which reached the surface of the earth or have been absorbed in the atmosphere.
- Changes in the movement of the earth in orbit. Slight shifts in the earth's angle of tilt, the earth's orbit pattern around the sun and changes in the gravitational influences of the sun and moon on the earth have all contributed to significant changes in the temperature pattern.
- Gases given off from rotting vegetation in tundra areas have affected global temperatures.

Human reasons:
- The testing of atom bombs releasing dust particles may have affected the earth's atmospheric conditions.
- The wide-scale burning of fossil fuels and forested areas throughout the world has released various chemicals into the air including sulphur dioxide, carbon monoxide and carbon dioxide.
- Trees, which gave out valuable oxygen to the air, have been cut down and removed in great quantities. This has inevitably disrupted the balance of gases within the atmosphere and has affected the processes involved in the earth's insolation patterns.
- Increasing industrialisation releasing air pollution from chimneys and factories.
- The increasing release of pollutants from traffic, rubbish dumps or other similar sources.
- Increase in gases such as methane from large herds of livestock, particularly cattle.

The above changes to the balance of gases in the Earth's atmosphere have greatly contributed to the phenomenon known as the 'Greenhouse Effect'. In addition to nitrogen and oxygen there is a small but important number of gases which contribute to the process of heating and retaining heat within the atmosphere. The gases responsible for the Greenhouse Effect include carbon dioxide, methane and fluorocarbons.

These gases help to allow short wave radiation back into space or absorb long wave radiation leaving the earth and to re-radiate it back to the surface. Without these gases temperatures at the earth's surface could fall dramatically by perhaps 10 to 15°C. If the level of gases increases this could led to a rise in temperature globally within the earth.

The ozone layer lies about 10 to 50 km from the Earth's surface and is very important since it acts as a shield against ultra-violet radiation from the sun. Releases of CFCs (chlorofluorocarbons) from, for example, aerosols and refrigerants, have reacted with gases in the ozone layer causing thinning or gaps known as the 'ozone hole'. The human effects of this change in the atmosphere include increases in rates of skin cancers and cataracts and reduced crop yields. Note that the ozone hole does not cause the Greenhouse Effect.

REGIONAL SCALE – EQUATORIAL AND SAVANNA REGIONS OF AFRICA

Key Point 14

You should be able to describe and explain the origin, nature and weather characteristics of Tropical Maritime (mT) and Tropical Continental (cT) air masses which affect West Africa

Air Masses

- Air masses are widespread expanses of homogenous air that are travelling in a horizontal direction. They are termed homogenous because the temperature and humidity levels of the air mass are similar throughout the surface layers. Horizontally they can measure up to hundreds of kilometres across. Areas where the air masses are created are called 'source regions'. The surface areas where uniform conditions are found (such as in areas of sub-tropical high pressure zones) are the most suitable locations for the development of air masses.

- The same can be said for polar and large continental regions. Some masses are extremely thick and extend upwards into the stratosphere. The air masses tend to migrate away from their source and, although travelling great distances, they can still retain many of the original physical properties in terms of temperature and humidity of their source regions.

- If the air mass originates in a warm, dry area (e.g. over a desert) it will bring those kinds of conditions to the areas over which it passes. If it originates over water areas, the air mass will bring wetter conditions.

- The masses are generally termed Maritime M or Continental C depending on whether they originated over sea or land respectively.

- They are also denoted as either Polar, Tropical or Arctic. They are denoted as mT or cT with the small letter indicating maritime or continental origin and the large letter showing the source region. It is quite normal to assume that tropical air masses include any air which has it source in the equatorial regions.

Key Point 15

You should know about inter-tropical convergence zones and 'Convergence and Divergence' as shown in Figure 1·7

January

July

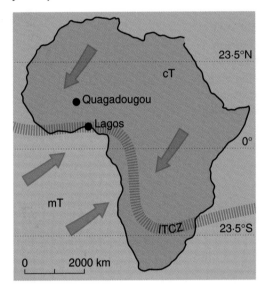
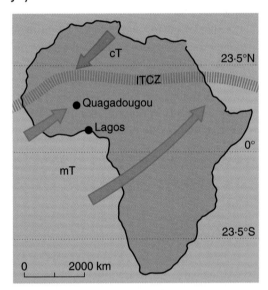

Figure 1·7 – Selected air masses and fronts over Africa – January and July

- A zone of convergence is where winds meet and a zone of divergence is an area where the winds go in different directions. Converging winds include the trade winds which meet at the equator in a zone termed the inter-tropical convergence zone (ITCZ). Winds which flow southwards from the polar areas converge with air flowing poleward from the sub-tropical high belts. Convergence of easterlies with the westerlies occurs along the polar front.

- Two zones of divergence occur in the sub-tropical high pressure zones where the winds are usually fairly light. The zones are referred to as the *'horse latitudes'*. Climatic conditions of the horse latitudes therefore consist generally of clear skies, abundant sunshine, low rainfall and calm or very light variable winds.

- In these zones, and in the ITCZ, the movement of air is vertical or convectional. In the ITCZ the air tends to rise along the inter-tropical front. The zone of convergence moves northwards and southwards with changes in the sun's angle of declination during the seasons. This shift in the ITCZ affects the climate of areas in these latitudes, especially rainfall patterns.

- When air masses from different source regions meet, the air at the edge begins a process in which the colder air forces warm air upward and condensation takes place in the upper parts. The place where this occurs is called the *front*.

- Where the trade wind belt of the northern latitudes meets the trade wind belt of the southern latitudes within the equatorial belt an inter-tropical front is formed. The weather associated with this front very much depends on whether the front has formed over the oceans or the continents. Air masses converging towards the inter-tropical front over oceans are moist in the lower layers and relatively dry at higher levels. At convergence there is some instability and large cumulus clouds appear; eventually this leads to intense shower and thunder conditions.
- Within equatorial areas the vertical movement of air through convection produces convectional rain. This belt of equatorial rainfall moves north or south with the annual changes in the sun's declination of about 5° latitude either side of the equator. The climate of equatorial Africa is therefore best described as high rainfall throughout the year with high temperatures with a small annual temperature range as shown in Figure 1·8.

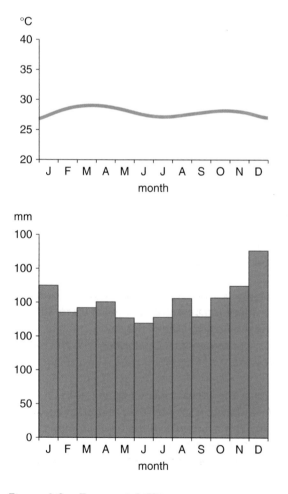

Figure 1·8 – Equatorial Climate

The variations are influenced by the following factors:
- In the northern hemisphere from March to July the ITCZ moves northwards across West Africa. This brings wetter conditions of convectional rain and clusters of clouds, which can become cumulonimbus clouds, bringing heavy rainfall.
- This rainy season lasts only about 2 months. At the northern edge conditions are much drier where the air meets dry air from the interior of the continent with its continental tropical air mass.
- As the ITCZ moves further southwards in winter, the drier continental tropical air is drawn southwards giving drier conditions in the north western areas.
- In some years there has been an apparent shift in the movement of the ITCZ which has resulted in less rainfall than normal in the areas north of the equator.
- This, combined with a southward extension of the sub-tropical high pressure from the Sahara, has resulted in long periods of drought.

GEOGRAPHICAL METHODS AND TECHNIQUES

Key Point 20
You should know the following geographical techniques:
How to construct climate graphs

You will not be asked to construct climate graphs in the external examination. The technique basically consists of plotting average monthly temperatures from January to December for any given place on a graph with an appropriate temperature scale, depending on the range of the temperatures given in the data.

Once plotted, these points are joined by a smooth line to indicate the trend in the temperature during the period of the year. This is a line graph.

Total monthly rainfall figures are plotted on the same graph from January to December in a series of bars. The scale chosen will again depend on the total amounts to be shown. The scale is usually shown on the left hand side of the graph in degrees celcius and on the right hand side in millimetres of precipitation.

How to describe and explain climate graphs

Describing a graph involves comments on the temperature and rainfall patterns throughout the year.

Temperature:
- Note the highest and lowest temperatures and the difference between them namely, the temperature range.
- Note the warmest and coolest periods of the year.
- Note whether there are definite seasons as indicated by temperatures.
- Note whether the climate is cold, cool, temperate, warm or hot.

Rainfall:
- Note the distribution of rainfall across the year and when the wettest and driest seasons occur.
- Note the amounts of rainfall in each month, indicating the general pattern, e.g. wet, dry, very dry.
- Note the overall amount of rainfall throughout the year indicating the overall pattern, e.g. very wet, moderate, dry etc.
- From your knowledge of different climate graphs from areas across the world, you should be able to identify a climate from a given graph, particularly equatorial and savanna climates.

SAMPLE QUESTIONS, ANSWERS, COMMENTS AND MARKING INSTRUCTIONS

Question 1

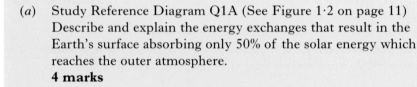

Reference Diagram Q1A

(*a*) Study Reference Diagram Q1A (See Figure 1·2 on page 11) Describe and explain the energy exchanges that result in the Earth's surface absorbing only 50% of the solar energy which reaches the outer atmosphere.
4 marks

(*b*) Study Reference Diagram Q1B (See Figure 1·3 on page 13) Explain how the circulation cells A, B and C and the related surface winds assist in the distribution of energy over the Earth.
5 marks
(9 marks)

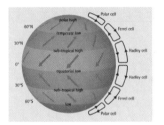

Reference Diagram Q1B

Sample answer – 1(*a*)
✓ denotes correct point

The incoming short-wave energy (insolation) from the sun is absorbed and reflected on its way to and by the earth.

26% of the energy is reflected back into space ✓ by the atmosphere. This could be due to dust and gases reflecting it ✓. 18% of the energy is absorbed by the atmosphere ✓. This could be due to other dust particles and gases retaining the energy ✓.

This leaves 56% which travels to the earth's surface ✓. Not all of this is absorbed either, with 6% of the energy being reflected by polar ice caps ✓. This means only 50% of the insolation is actually absorbed by the earth.

Comments and marks obtained – 1(*a*)
The first statement receives no marks since it simply restates the question.
The second paragraph contains four relevant points which merit $\frac{1}{2}$ mark each. These include the calculation of 26% of energy reflected back and the reason for this, namely that it is reflected back by dust and gases. The second two $\frac{1}{2}$ marks are obtained from the statement on the absorption of 18% of energy by dust particles and gases, although the reference to 'other particles and gases' is less accurate.
The final two $\frac{1}{2}$ marks are obtained from the statement noting that of the 56% of energy travelling to the earth's surface, 6% is reflected back by the polar ice caps.
The final statement again repeats the information given in the question and therefore gains no further marks.
In total, the answer is good enough to obtain 3 marks out of a possible 4.
A solid pass.

Sample answer – 1(b)

The cells A,B,C and the surface winds help to distribute energy over the earth by circulation of air. Cell A is called the Hadley Cell ✓. It is driven directly by the rising hot air at the equator ✓. This warm air travels to the tropics where it falls.

Cell C is the Polar Cell ✓. It is also driven directly, but this time by falling cold air at the poles ✓. This cold air falls and travels to l latitudes around 60° ✓ where it is heated and rises.

Cell B, the Ferrel Cell ✓ is driven indirectly. It is driven by the downwards. action of falling air at the tropics and rising air at around 60 ✓. The resulting winds circulate the air over the surface.

Comments and marks obtained – 1(b)

The marks in this answer are obtained from correctly identifying the three cells shown in the reference diagram – each gaining $\frac{1}{2}$ mark. Further $\frac{1}{2}$ marks are obtained by the references to 'hot air rising', 'falling cold air at the poles' and 'falling and rising air at the tropics and around 60°. 'Two further $\frac{1}{2}$ marks would be obtained for the references to the movement of the 'warm air to the tropics' and cold air travelling to latitudes at around 60°. Further marks could have been obtained had there been any references to earth movement or the influence of jet streams or Rossby waves and perhaps a more detailed explanation of the movement of air, particularly in the mid-latitudes. The answer nevertheless is good enough to obtain a pass of 4 marks out of a possible 5.

Sample answer – 2(c)

There are several reasons for the variation in global temperature as shown below.

1) In the 1900s there was a bigger increase in industry. These were mainly smoke stack industry causing a lot of pollution ✓. Resulting in global warming ✓ where energy that is reflected cannot get past the thick polluted atmosphere ✓ and is sent back to earth.

2) Another reason is an increase in cars ✓. The number of cars is increasing at an alarming rate causing more pollution and adding to the global warming. This pollution is also affecting a layer called the ozone layer which did help keep out much of the sun's unwanted rays but all the pollution is making holes in it and letting more energy through ✓.

3) With quite a big demand for wood and land for farming people are chopping down rainforests and burning the wood ✓.

4) Some people think the temperatures are part of a cycle and they will naturally increase until returning to normal in around a hundred years time ✓.

5) More people are using CFCs which gives off another dangerous gas that damages the ozone layer ✓.

6) Before 1900 there was less industry, fewer cars and CFCs so the temperatures were lower ✓.

Comments and marks obtained – 2(c)

By attempting this part of the question, the candidate has made a fundamental mistake, often made by other candidates in the examination. By failing to properly read the instruction at the beginning of the question, the candidate has answered three parts – (a), (b), and (c) when only two answers were required. The candidate may therefore have lost valuable time writing an unnecessary answer.

The answer to part (c) however, is a very good answer and is worth more marks than that given to part (b).

The marks for part (c) would therefore be counted in preference to those obtained for part (b).

The references to 'smoke stack industries', 'global warming' and 'energy reflected back to earth' would obtain $3 \times \frac{1}{2}$ marks. The further comments on 'increase in cars' and the 'chopping down of rain forests', would gain two more $\frac{1}{2}$ marks. The further reference to pollution affecting the ozone layer might gain a further $\frac{1}{2}$ mark. The comments on the 'temperature cycle' in part 4 and CFCs in part 5 merit two additional $\frac{1}{2}$ marks.

In total, the answer has sufficient explanatory point to obtain the maximum marks available, namely $4\frac{1}{2}$ out of 4 although only a maximum of 4 marks are available.

In total this gives the answer $7\frac{1}{2}$ marks out of 8. An excellent, high A grade pass.

Question 3

(a) Study Reference Map Q3A (See Figure 1·7 on page 20)
Describe the origin and weather characteristics of the Tropical
Maritime and Tropical Continental air masses.
4 marks

(b) Study Reference Maps Q3A and Q3B (See Figure 1·7 on page 20)
Using the maps and graphs, describe and explain the pattern of
annual rainfall in both the north and south of Nigeria.
5 marks

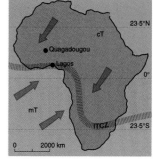

Reference Diagram Q3A

Sample answer – 3(a)

The tropical maritime air mass originates over the Atlantic Ocean ✓ and is
very moist and warm ✓. When it blows over the Atlantic Ocean it lets some
of the water from the Atlantic evaporate and move with it when it moves
towards Africa ✓.
The continental maritime air mass originates over land ✓ and this makes it a
very dry and warm air mass ✓. It does not blow over much water and a lot of
land therefore it becomes very dry ✓.
The tropical maritime air mass brings with it rainy and warm ✓ conditions.
The tropical continental brings with it dry and warm ✓ conditions.

Reference Diagram Q3B

Comments and marks obtained – 3(a)

The opening sentence would gain three $\frac{1}{2}$ marks for the correct references to the
origin and characteristics of the tropical maritime air mass (Atlantic Ocean, warm
and moist). Similarly the reference to the continental (but not maritime) air mass
originating over land and being warm and dry would obtain three further $\frac{1}{2}$ marks.
The final correct references to the types of weather associated with both air
masses ('rainy/warm' and 'dry/warm') merit two further $\frac{1}{2}$ marks each.
In total the answer would gain 4 marks out of 4. An excellent, high quality answer.

Sample answer – 3(b)

In January, Kano which is in the north of Nigeria has a very dry winter ✓
which is because the tropical continental air mass is over them and this brings
with it very dry conditions ✓. The reason for this is that it has blown over
the desert and lost any moisture it may have had. In July Kano has over
250mm of rainfall ✓. This will be caused by the tropical maritime air mass
✓ which is very wet because it has travelled over the Atlantic Ocean bringing
with it wet conditions ✓. It is only over for four months or so and the wet
conditions don't last long.
In January Enugu which is in the south of Nigeria has a relatively dry winter
✓. This is again because the continental air mass is overhead bringing with it
dry conditions ✓.
In July, Enugu has a very, very wet summer ✓. This again will be because the
tropical maritime air mass is over head bringing with it very wet conditions ✓.
This area may even experience some flash floods because of the moisture. The
tropical maritime will not have lost any rain on to land before it gets to Nigeria

Comments and marks obtained 3(b)

This is a very high quality answer, which follows the instruction in the question to both describe and explain the pattern of annual rainfall. Good use is made of the maps and diagrams provided and this is incorporated into the answer throughout as the candidate attempts to describe the pattern.

Marks would be obtained for correctly identifying the dry winter in the north of Nigeria caused by the tropical continental air mass – two $\frac{1}{2}$ marks.

Reference to the 250mm of rainfall in Kano in July, caused by the tropical maritime air mass and short rainy season 'only for four months', would obtain a further three $\frac{1}{2}$ marks. Comments on the dry winter in Enugu caused by the continental air mass bringing dry conditions gains another two $\frac{1}{2}$ marks.

Finally, the description of Enugu's very wet summer and the explanatory reference to the tropical maritime air mass gains two more $\frac{1}{2}$ marks.

Unfortunately there is no reference to the ITCZ by way of explanation.

This gives a total of $4\frac{1}{2}$ marks out of 5. A very high quality answer.

Marking instructions

When using the marking instructions for all sample questions note the following.

The marking instructions provided in this text give a guide as to the kind of instructions which might be issued to a Marker by the SQA.

Each correct statement would probably be awarded a $\frac{1}{2}$ mark.

Although the instructions contain a variety of answers, not all statements are necessary for full marks, nor are these statements meant to be an exclusive list of correct answers.

Question 1

1(a) Assess out of 4. Answers may include points such as:

There is more concentrated sun on tropical latitudes as the intensity of insolation is greatest where the sun's rays strike vertically. Less atmosphere passed through at the equator. There are more direct rays, therefore less solar radiation is lost through reflection. Surfaces at the equator are more likely to absorb radiation, e.g. rainforests. The variation in insolation changes with seasons at the poles, e.g. six months of polar darkness. Reference to the albedo effect.

1(b) Assess out of 5. Credit should be given for any diagrams which enhance the answer.

Candidates must describe the transfer of energy from low to high latitudes.

Answers may include reference to:

Net heating in low latitudes results in rising air around the equator which moves toward the poles and sinks at higher latitudes. The creation of Hadley Cells – with warm moist air rising above the equator creating thunderstorms and releasing heat into the upper atmosphere.

Cells also include air at ground level moving between sub-tropics and equator to replace rising air, i.e. sinking of air at sub-tropical high pressure belts and the return of air via the North-east and South-east trade winds. Mid-latitude westerlies which develop from the poleward side of sub-tropical high pressure zone. Jet Stream (i.e. fast moving winds at higher altitudes) which are a mechanism for the mixing of air of different temperatures and therefore allow the transfer of energy.

Question 2

2(a) Answers which fail to provide a diagram would be assessed out of 3.

With the aid of a suitably annotated diagram, answers should refer to:

The sun's rays being more concentrated on tropical / equatorial latitudes where the rays strike vertically. Consequently the intensity of insolation is greatest in these areas. Less solar radiation is lost at tropical latitudes due to the sun's rays being more direct.

Due to the different curvature of the earth's surface at the tropics and the poles, the rays have less atmosphere to pass through at the tropics than at the poles.

The angle of the sun in the sky decreases towards the poles and therefore the same amount of heat is spread over a larger area than at the tropics.

There are different relative albedos between the tropics and the poles. The darker forest cover on surfaces near the equator absorb more radiation whereas the lighter snow covered surfaces at the poles reflect incoming solar radiation.

2(b) Marks would probably be allocated on the basis of 2 for description and 2 for explanation.

Descriptive points might include:

In the *north Atlantic* the circulatory pattern is *clockwise* (e.g. the Gulf stream / North Atlantic Drift, Caribbean Current and the warm North Equatorial Current).

In the *south Atlantic* the pattern is *anticlockwise* (e.g. the warm Brazilian Current which originates in the tropical latitudes and returns towards the equator off the coasts of Namibia and Angola as the cold Benguela Current).

Explanation might include points such as:

The relationship between currents and prevailing winds; energy is transferred through friction between the wind and currents. Huge areas in both the Atlantic and Pacific Oceans encourage the development of the gyre or theoretical loop controlled by sub-tropical high pressure cells. The continents deflect currents (e.g. the West Wind Drift). The Coriolis effect – whereby winds are deflected to the right in the northern hemisphere and to the left in the southern hemisphere – is greatly influential. Density differences result from differential heating in the oceans causing chilled water to sink to the ocean floor and to spread towards the equator (as in the case of the Labrador Current).

2(c) Since the question requires candidates to 'suggest reasons' for variations in global temperatures, descriptive points are unnecessary although most answers will include some element of description.

Any descriptive points included in an answer would probably gain no more than a maximum of one mark.

The reasons suggested might include factors such as: variations in solar energy; astronomical cycles (involving for example periodic variations in the Earth's tilt or orbit path); impact of increasing pollution in the Earth's atmosphere; increase in the amount of greenhouse gases due to burning of forests, traffic fumes, burning of fossil fuels – all producing an increase in carbon dioxide; increase in CFCs from aerosols, refrigerators and foam packaging. Other factors could include methane given off from marshland, manure, livestock (especially cattle), rice padi fields and various other sources. Exhaust from vehicles, power stations and agricultural fertilisers which produce nitrous oxides which are released into the atmosphere.

Question 3

Credit would be given for the definition of an air mass. Each air mass described would be awarded 2 marks.

3(*a*)

Tropical maritime air mass

Originates over the Atlantic Ocean in tropical latitudes.

It is warm, moist and unstable. Main characteristics include – hot / very hot weather and very humid with 65 – 82% relative humidity.

Tropical continental air mass

Originates over the Sahara Desert (i.e. a large land mass in tropical latitudes).

It is warm and dry with stable air; it brings very warm dry air in winter and extremely hot, dry weather in summer. Relative humidity is low 10 – 17%.

3(*b*) Usually answers that simply describe without giving explanation would probably obtain no more than 2 marks out of 5.

Answers should refer to the seasonal pattern with 7 months dry and 5 months rain with intense rain during rainy season.

Explanation would refer to:

Changing location of overhead sun during the year; dates of overhead sun; changes in wind direction; the source of the wind which causes dry conditions and the source of the wind bringing wet conditions.

GLOSSARY OF ASSOCIATED TERMS

Albedo – This refers to the amount of reflectability of surfaces on the earth such as land, ice and water.

Climate – This is the average conditions of weather usually taken over a period of 35 years.

Desert – Any area which has less than 250mm rainfall throughout the year. Note that there are cold and hot deserts in the world.

Doldrums – a comparable term for the ITCZ (inter-tropical convergence zone)

Drought – This occurs when there is a long period without rainfall. Notice that droughts do no necessarily just happen in desert areas.

Front – The boundary between two air masses. If the air on one mass is warmer than air being replaced the front is termed a warm front. If the air is colder than the air being replaced the front is termed a cold front.

Homogeneous Air Mass – A large volume of air which is composed of the same properties.

Insolation – Incoming solar radiation – insolation is the amount of heat taken in from the sun.

Intertropical front – Now referred to as the Inter Tropical Convergence Zone (ITCZ) since it was discovered that air converges not at a 'front' but in a broad zonal trough of low pressure in equatorial latitudes.

Jet Streams – A narrrow belt of high altitude (above 12000 metres) westerly winds in the troposphere.

Latitude – This is the distance between the equator and the poles and is measured in degrees.

Rainfall pattern – This refers to the distribution of rainfall throughout the year for example, rainfall may occur mainly in certain times of the year, e.g. winter or summer or be spread evenly throughout the year.

Pressure belts – Patterns of atmospheric circulation systems of either high or low atmospheric pressure.

Range of Temperature – This is the difference between the highest temperature and the lowest temperature in a year.

Rossby waves – A smooth wave shape undulation in the airflow in the middle and upper troposphere.

Solar energy – Any form of energy originating from the sun.

Troposphere – The lowest layer of the earth's concentric layers of atmoshpere ranging in altitude from about 18 km at the equator to 6 km at the poles.

Tundra – This region lies between the polar region of perpetual snow and ice and the northern limit of tree growth in the northern hemisphere, and is usually referred to as a cold desert area.

HYDROSPHERE

Hydrology is the study of the Earth's water, whether it is in the atmosphere, on the surface or underground. The movement of that water, the impact of it on the land and how this movement may be interrupted are also important aspects of this particular topic.

HYDROLOGICAL CYCLE

Key Point 1

You should be able to both draw a diagram to show the global hydrological cycle and be able to describe the main elements of the diagram

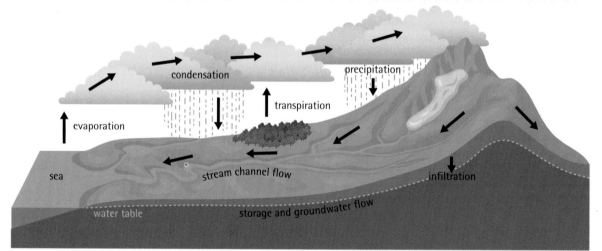

Figure 2·1 Hydrological cycle

1. Water exists on the surface in the form of oceans, seas, lakes, rivers and streams. It also exists in the atmosphere as rain and water vapour and underground as seepage within rock structures and in underground streams and lakes. The surface water can pass into the atmosphere through evaporation and can be carried by winds and eventually returns to the surface as rain or snow.
2. Water also exists on the surface as ice or snow, e.g. at the poles or in high altitudes. Water on the land may be returned to oceans and seas through rivers or streams. This intricate process of the movement of water back and forward between land, oceans and the atmosphere is called the hydrological cycle.
3. The hydrological cycle works as a closed system in that there is a definite amount of water in the atmosphere, lithosphere and hydrosphere (land and water areas). This amount remains constant.
4. The system is powered by energy from the sun. Within the system the amount of water in the various components can and does vary, especially when the system is interrupted.

Key Point 2

You should be able to explain how balance is maintained within the hydrological cycle. Although the amounts referred to in Key Point 1 remain constant, there is a continuous movement of water between the different parts of the system through the processes of evaporation, transpiration and precipitation

- Of the 1360 million km³ of water in the world, 1322 million km³ (97·2%) is contained in the oceans. The remainder is split between the ice caps and glaciers, groundwater (sub-surface water) surface water in the form of lakes, rivers and streams and a small percentage – 0·04% is in the atmosphere.
- A balance is maintained within the system. Water evaporating from the oceans is balanced by water being returned through precipitation and surface run-off.
- The balance is affected if there are changes to the basic system through for example, interruption in the run-off through water storage systems such as dams or changes in world temperature patterns (including the greenhouse effect).
- Evaporation and precipitation rates vary widely across the world. The energy that creates evaporation comes from the sun.
- Areas where temperatures are high, e.g. equatorial and tropical areas, have high evaporation rates, especially over the oceans. The rate of evaporation is also assisted by winds. Warm winds help water to evaporate more than cold calm conditions.
- Areas which have dry conditions (such as deserts) have relatively low evaporation rates since there is very little surface water to evaporate.

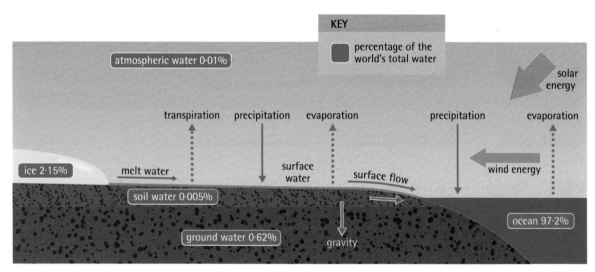

Figure 2·2 Water balance throughout the world

FLUVIAL LANDFORMS AND LANDSCAPES

Key Point 3
Using an O.S. map, you should be able to describe the main characteristics of a river and its valley

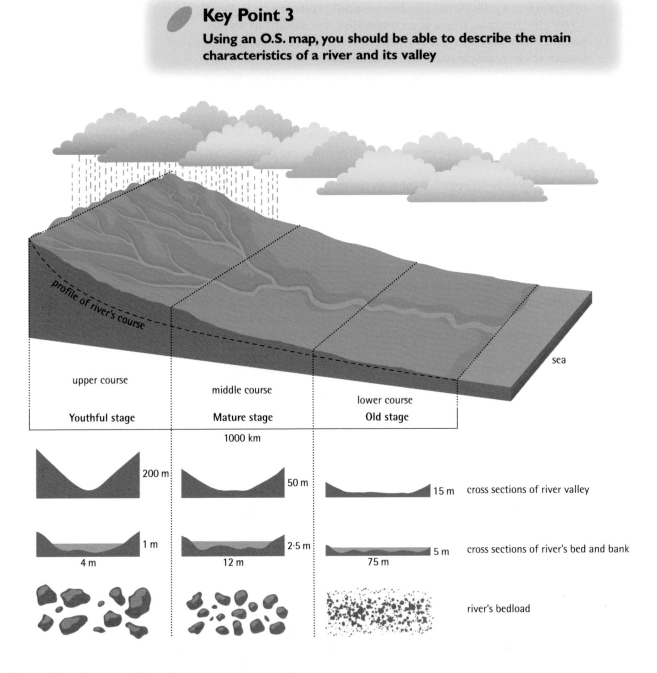

Figure 2·3 – Section of river from source to mouth

The basic system of surface drainage is known as a **river basin.**

This consists of a complex interaction of components which include rainfall, channel run-off, surface streams, soils, slope, solar energy, groundwater storage, evaporation from surface and evapotranspiration from vegetation.

The system returns water to the oceans and seas as part of the hydrological cycle.

When describing the features of a river and its valley on an O.S. map refer to:
- The stage of development of the valley, e.g. *young*, *mature* or *old* as determined from the contour patterns of the valley.
- Direction of flow as indicated by both contour lines and spot heights at various points along the course.
- The gradient should be described (steep or gentle) using spot heights and contours as a basis for deciding on steepness.
- Distinct features within the valley, e.g. meanders, tributaries, ox-bow lakes, floodplain width should be mentioned. Refer only to physical features and not human features such as bridges, roads or settlements.
- If referring to certain physical features, give appropriate 4 or 6 figure grid references.

Key Point 4

You should be able to explain the formation of selected physical features of a river and its valley

These features might include the following: the stage of development, waterfalls, meanders, flood plains, braiding and ox-bow lakes.

Stage of development

- River valleys can take different shapes, often depending on their stage of development.
- In the early stage of development or *Youthful stage*, the gradient (or slope) is usually very steep and the river is fast flowing. The sides of the valley will be steep and at this stage the main work of the river is usually erosion.
- The erosion process is greatest during periods of heavy rainfall. The river has more energy to affect the bedload, and material is rolled and bounced along. Downward or vertical erosion occurs and the valley takes on the characteristic V-shape.
- The steepness of the valley at this stage is also greatly influenced by factors such as local climate, rock type and local vegetation which can affect chemical erosion. As the river is forced to wind its path due to variations in the relief and rock type, features called interlocking spurs are formed.
- If a river flows over hard rock and then over a band of less resistant rock in a waterfall, the less resistant rock will be worn away much more quickly than the overlying rock. This happens because the velocity increases as the river drops allowing the river to erode the weaker rock. Eventually so much of the underlying rock may be eroded that there will nothing left to support the rock above. The overlying rock then collapses. As the process is repeated the waterfall will retreat and this may eventually lead to the formation of a gorge. A gorge is a deep valley with very steep sides and a narrow valley floor.
- In the middle and later stages of a river's development, the valley sides are less steep and the gradient is more gentle. The width of the river increases and bends or meanders begin to form.

Meanders

In the middle stage of the valley (the *Mature stage* of a river's development), the valley sides are less steep although they may still be hilly. The gradient becomes more gentle and the width of the valley increases with an increase in flat land along the sides of the river.

River bends or meanders begin to appear as the river finds the course of least resistance. The speed of flow of the river varies across the meander. The rate of flow is much faster on the outside bend of the meander and at this point the water is eroding the outer bank.

On the inside bend the velocity is slower and the river begins to deposit its load. In the lower or final stage of the valley (corresponding to the *Old stage* in a river's development) the river widens and flows more slowly across the land. The river flood plain usually increases in width and large meanders are common.

Braiding

Material may be deposited in the middle of a river channel, forming islands. This process is known as braiding. The islands of deposited material divided by the different channels are called 'eyots'.

As the size of meanders increase, eventually the river may cut a channel between the narrowest point of the bends – the feature which is left cut off from the river is called an *oxbow lake*.

Key Point 5

You should be able to explain the effects of flowing water in relation to the processes of erosion, transportation and deposition in each of the three stages of a river valley

Effects of flowing water

As water flows downwards under the force of gravity it follows the path of least resistance. As rivers flow, three separate processes take place. The first of these is erosion.

Erosion is the wearing away of the land surface over which the river flows. This wearing away occurs in different ways. It occurs through processes such as abrasion, hydraulic action, corrosion and attrition.

- *Abrasion* happens when small particles of rock carried by the river rub the suface of the river bed and wear away its surface. This process increases with the speed of the river.
- Water flowing past river banks can be forced into cracks in the river bank and after some time the banks can collapse. This process, which is more gradual than abrasion, is called *hydraulic action*.
- *Attrition* occurs when water flow causes pieces of rock to collide and break up.
- *Corrosion* is caused by chemical reactions between carbonic acid or acid from vegetation and the river bed.

Transportation is the second process which is carried out by rivers.
- The material which is eroded by the processes outlined above is carried or transported by the river and this material is called the river's load. The rate of transportation is related to the energy of the river which in turn is related to the volume and speed of the river.
- The rock type over which the river flows will also affect the river's ability to transport material, since different rocks will offer different rates of resistance and therefore the amount of interruption to the flow will vary.

Deposition occurs when the velocity of the river begins to decrease. When this happens the river no longer has the competence to carry all of its load.
- If a river overflows its banks during a flood, material is deposited creating a feature called the flood plain. Occasionally the load of a river may be increased due to for example a landslide caused by heavy rainfall. The ability of the river to transport the overall load is reduced and therefore deposition takes place.

Key Point 6

You should be able to explain how soil water and groundwater storage varies according to changes in precipitation, evaporation, transpiration, infiltration and local geology

The main characteristics of the drainage basin system

- **Inputs** refers to the water which is put into the system through precipitation
  Outputs refers to the water which is lost to the system either by the river and its tributaries returning it to the sea or by evapotranspiration.
  Evapotranspiration is the combined return of water to the atmosphere by evaporation and transpiration. *Evaporation* is the water loss from the ground or water surfaces because of the heating effect of the sun. *Transpiration* is water loss from vegetation through leaf pores.
- Stored water is water held within the drainage basin system in lakes or in the soil. Water transfer refers to water percolating or infiltrating through the rock strata. The return of that water may be interrupted by some being absorbed by soils and by vegetation such as trees.
- Each basin is separated from neighbouring basins by a *watershed*. This feature is the area of high ground that divides basins where the surface water flows in different directions.
- During periods of heavy rainfall or low temperatures the soil and sub-soil may become saturated or impenetrable, resulting in an increase in surface run-off. Similarly if rainfall is low, certain flow channels may become dry if the soil is permeable.
- The absorption of water is known as *infiltration*. Soils which have become compacted through for example, overgrazing, may also become more impermeable and therefore surface run-off will increase.

Key Point 9

You should be able to compare hydrographs for two different river basins

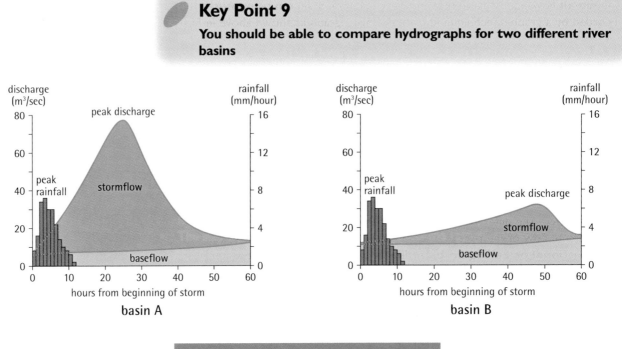

basin A

basin B

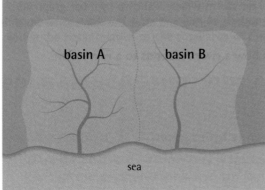

Figure 2·5 – Two selected flood hydrographs / river basins

Analysis

- Drainage basin A has a much higher density than that of drainage basin B. Comparison of the hydrographs for each basin shows that for basin A the lag time is much shorter (30 hours) than basin B (55 hours).
- The peak discharge for A is much higher (140 cumecs) than basin B (50 cumecs).
- The rising limb for B is less steep than for A, as is the recession (falling) limb.
- Apart from the difference in density of drainage within the two basins, it is quite possible that there is some considerable variation in the relief pattern where the pattern may be much steeper in basin A than B.
- The the soil and rock types may also vary thereby affecting the overland flow patterns and perhaps the throughflow patterns.
- Further analysis might reveal that there are some differences between the vegetation present within the two basins. For example there may be more woodland present in B than A which will affect discharge.

- The net result of these differences in hydrographs and basin characteristics is that the river in basin A is more likely to flood than the river within basin B.
- Note however, without more detail on the characteristics of both systems flood predictions are speculative.

> **Key Point 10**
> In addition to being able to describe and explain hydrographs, you should be able to note the effects that changes to a drainage system, such as an increase in vegetation or steepness of slope or the presence of permeable or impermeable rock, could have on different graphs

- Hydrographs are affected by the area of the basin since the larger the basin size the greater the discharge. The amount of the discharge is also related to the amount of rainfall. Therefore the peak flow will be higher in larger basins.
- If the slopes are steep, the rate of infiltration will be lower and therefore the peak flow will be greater. If the basin has flatter slopes, there will be more infiltration and this will result in lower peaks.
- The lag time is also affected by steepness of slope: the steeper the slope, the shorter the lag time.
- Quickflow will increase where the rainfall is high and the infiltration is low. The discharge will also be affected by local vegetation, the number of tributary streams and whether the drainage basin has been affected by human land use.
- Towns and city hydrographs are different to those of rural environments since there will be many more impermeable surface areas such as pavements and roads, surface drains and gutters. There may also be less vegetation to interrupt the run-off.

SAMPLE QUESTIONS, ANSWERS, COMMENTS AND MARKING INSTRUCTIONS

Question 1

(a) Study Reference Diagram Q1A (See below)
Describe and explain the hydrographs for the River Severn and the River Wye after the storm of 6 August 1973.
4 marks

(b) Study Reference Diagram Q1B (See below)
Select one of the flood plain features shown and, with the aid of a diagram or diagrams, describe and explain its nature and formation.
4 marks

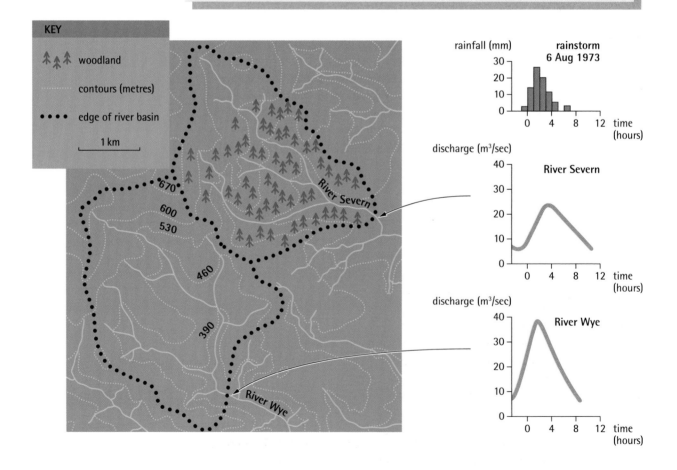

Reference Diagram Q1 A – Hydrographs of the Rivers Severn and Wye

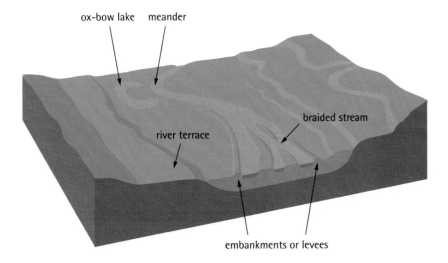

ox-bow lake   meander

braided stream

river terrace

embankments or levees

Reference Diagram Q1B – Features of a flood plain

Sample answer – 1(a)
✓ **denotes correct point**

> The river Severn basin is covered by woodland ✓. This would delay the water from reaching the river basin as quickly as the water ✓ in the Wye basin as this is not covered by vegetation. The woodland and vegetation would stop the water from running down the valley sides quickly and also some would be taken up by the roots ✓. This accounts for the longer delay time at the beginning of the river Severn's hydrograph ✓. The vegetation is also responsible for the lower height reached by the Severn— 23 m³/s compared to the high 47 m³/s in the Wye basin ✓. The River Severn's drainage basin is also situated on gentler slopes than the Wye. This factor also reduces the runoff in the Severn's basin ✓. The river Wye takes a shorter period of time, however, to return to its normal discharge level — about 9 hours ✓. this is due to the water being held back longer in the Severn's basin.

Comments and marks obtained – 1(a)

The first part of the answer correctly compares the basins' rates of discharge and relates them to the presence of woodland in the River Severn's basin, thus gaining two $\frac{1}{2}$ marks. The reference to lack of vegetation in the Wye basin is not correct. The answer then tends to repeat the explanation of the impact of the woodland although the point about the tree roots taking up water would receive an additional $\frac{1}{2}$ mark. A further $\frac{1}{2}$ mark is obtained by relating this last point to the delay time in the River Severn's hydrograph.

The answer makes references to the discharge rates, using data from the graphs although the reference to 47 m³/sec for the Wye basin is incorrect. This obtains a further $\frac{1}{2}$ mark. There are no marks for the statement on the slopes of the Severn basin since the contour pattern on the map does not confirm this.

Two final $\frac{1}{2}$ marks are obtained for the descriptive points relating to the shorter time for the Wye to return to its normal discharge, again using correct calculations from the graphs.

In total the answer would probably merit $7 \times \frac{1}{2}$ marks, thus $3\frac{1}{2}$ marks out of a possible 4. A very good answer.

Sample answer – 1(b)

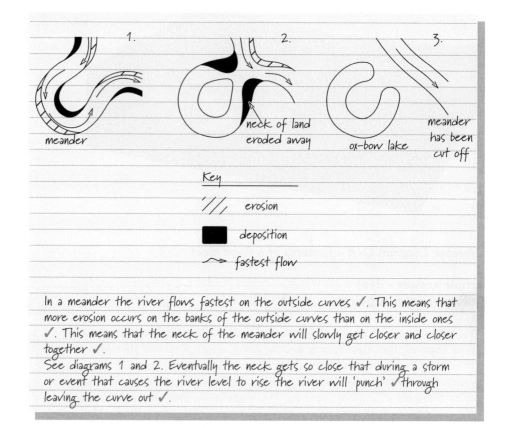

In a meander the river flows fastest on the outside curves ✓. This means that more erosion occurs on the banks of the outside curves than on the inside ones ✓. This means that the neck of the meander will slowly get closer and closer together ✓.

See diagrams 1 and 2. Eventually the neck gets so close that during a storm or event that causes the river level to rise the river will 'punch' ✓ through leaving the curve out ✓.

Comments and marks obtained – 1(b)

The first two comments on the speed of the river on the outside curves and the fact that erosion takes place on the outer bend are both worth $\frac{1}{2}$ mark each.

The reference to the neck becoming closer as shown in the diagram is worth a further $\frac{1}{2}$ mark.

The final marks are obtained from the remarks on the neck closing during a rise in river level and finally 'punching' through and isolating the curve.

The description of the formation process could have been a little more precise, especially in reference to the creation of the ox bow lake in the final stage.

Altogether the answer would probably merit $2\frac{1}{2}$ marks out of 4. Just above a basic pass.

Question 2

(*a*) Describe with the aid of a diagram, the global hydrological cycle.
5 marks

(*b*) Study Reference Diagram Q2 (see Figure 2·3 on page 38)
Choose one part of the river's course (upper or middle or lower),
and explain the effects of flowing water in terms of erosion,
transportation and deposition.
5 marks
(10 marks)

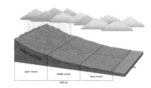

Reference Diagram Q2

Sample answer – 2(*a*)

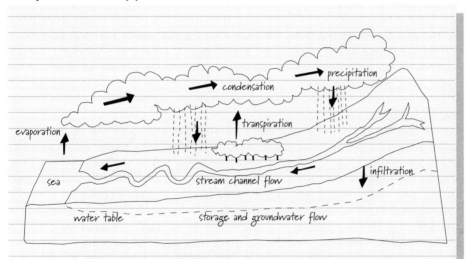

The earth contains a set amount of water which cannot be lowered by loss of
water, or heightened by gain of water ✓. The highest percentage of the
earth's water is that in seas and oceans (over 95%) with the second highest
percentage trapped in ice caps and at the poles ✓. The two main processes in
the hydrological cycle are evaporation and precipitation ✓. Water is evaporated
from the sea and forms rain clouds which will either release their water back
into the sea or lakes ✓, or will remain in clouds which will travel for a while
✓. The clouds release water as rainfall for a variety of reasons (e.g. relief
rainfall), and the rainwater that falls is either returned to the river or sea by
way of overland flow ✓, or is absorbed by the soil and travels by way of
throughflow (through the soil) back to the river or sea ✓. The slowest form
of water to return to its source is that of groundwater which takes a long
time due to the level to which it sinks ✓ (has to pass through porous or
pervious rock).
Only animals and plants (and other organisms) contribute to the hydrological cycle
by the processes of respiration ✓ (give out water vapour) and photosynthesis in
green plants (use water) ✓.

Comments and marks obtained – 2(a)

The answer is well structured and contains several good points. The first statement is a litle vague but is basically correct. The next reference to the make-up of the earth's water is also correct thus giving a total of one mark for the opening two sentences. The candidate identifies the processes of evaporation and precipitation and provides good examples of this and therefore obtains a further mark. The next two sentences would gain a further mark for describing how rainfall eventually returns to the sea with a good description of the process. The next statement on groundwater and the length of time involved in the process is good enough for a fourth mark. If a fifth mark was needed for full marks it would be given for the reference to plants and animals in the hydrological process.

In effect the answer has enough correct statements to gain 5 marks out of 5 for the question. An excellent well informed answer.

Sample answer – 2(b)

> In the upper course of the river, the most erosion occurs due to the large size of the river's bed load ✓. The water at this stage is flowing at a greater velocity ✓ than that of the other two stages, and is therefore able to 'pluck' large rocks from its banks ✓.
> The narrowness of the banks means a smaller surface area to be eroded ✓ results in high erosion ✓.
> These large rocks are rolled along the river floor and in doing so the rub and wear away the river bed (traction ✓). Slightly smaller rocks bounce along the river bed and can cause pot holes to be drilled in the bed ✓ and banks in certain conditions.
> In the upper course, the large rocks are worn down or broken up before meeting the middle course ✓. Only extremely large rocks are deposited at the earliest stage of the upper course ✓ due to the to the high velocity of the water. However, on meeting the middle course, the water deepens thus decreasing the river velocity ✓. As a result, deposition of the larger rocks occur.

Comments and marks obtained – 2(b)

This answer correctly describes the processes which take place in the upper stage of the river valley. All three processes, erosion, transportation and deposition are discussed.

The first paragraph gains marks for the references to the 'velocity of the water, plucking of rocks from the banks, giving $2 \times \frac{1}{2}$ marks.

Additional marks are obtained from the comments on the 'rolling of large rocks and the bouncing of rocks along the river bed causing further erosion' giving a further $2 \times \frac{1}{2}$ marks.

The final paragraph has sufficient comments to merit another $3 \times \frac{1}{2}$ for the references to the wearing down of the large rocks, the deepening of the river and its effect on river velocity.

The final comment on deposition is only partially accurate in that deposition does take place, but not of larger rocks.

The answer is worth possibly $3\frac{1}{2}$ to 4 out of 5 marks giving a total of $8\frac{1}{2}$ / 9 marks out of 10. A high quality answer.

Marking instructions

Question 1
(each correct statement would be awarded a $\frac{1}{2}$ mark).

Answers which simply describe would probably obtain no more than 2 marks.

1(a) Discharge in both rivers reaches a peak between 3 and 4 hours after the start of the storm. The maximum discharge from the River Severn is smaller and peaks later than the River Wye: this is due to the forest cover in the Severn basin slowing down infiltration rates and intercepting the rain as it falls.

After peaking, the discharge in the Severn basin falls more gradually due to the slower release of water into the river. Maximum discharge in the River Wye is greater than the Severn and peaks more steeply and more rapidly.

This is due to the moorland cover which permits faster infiltration of the rainfall and less interception by vegetation than in the Severn basin.

The discharge from the Wye rapidly decreases after it reaches its peak. There may also be reference to the relative steepness of the slopes in both basins.

1(b) Answers should contain both description and explanation of the selected feature.

Answers without diagrams would possibly gain a maximum of 3 out of 4 marks. For an oxbow lake points might include:

How the original meander developed; erosion taking place on the outer bend due to the faster flow of the river; deposition on the inside bend; gradual development of the meander to the point where the neck becomes narrower; eventually river joins up cutting a new path; leaving the former meander abandoned in a horseshoe shape – forming the oxbow lake.

Question 2
Mark out of 5. Each correct statement would be awarded a $\frac{1}{2}$ mark.

2(a) The answer should refer to the basic cycle of evaporation from the ocean; precipitation on to the land; run off back to the sea.

Reference could also be made to the majority of evaporation eventually being returned to the ocean. Precipitation on land goes into the soil and some held in groundwater; there is evaporation and transpiration from land and vegetation.

Answers without a diagram would probably gain no more than 3 marks out of 4.

A fully annotated diagram could obtain full marks.

2(b) The answer would be assessed out of 5 but the maximum of marks could be reduced by 1 mark for each process omitted. Answers should also refer only to the stage chosen for discussion.

Answers should clearly discuss the effects of flowing water in terms of: erosion; transportation; deposition. Named river features such as V-shaped valleys, meanders, oxbow lakes etc., would gain only a maximum of 1 mark.

Reference could be made for example to: velocity of the river; downward erosion; bed load material being transported; suspension; load; width and depth of the river; silt; flooding; type of movement of river material; gradient.

GLOSSARY OF ASSOCIATED TERMS

Aquifer: Permeable rocks that are storing groundwater

Evapotransiration: The process by which moistrure is returned to the atmosphere by direct means through evaporation combined with transpiration from vegetation.

Interlocking Spurs: The bottom part of slopes in a valley which intertwine.

Infiltration: The process by which water seeps into the soil and sub soil.

Hydrosphere: The name given to all of the water surfaces on the earth.

Lag time: A time delay between the arrival of a signal in a meteorlogical measuring instrument and the response of that instrument.

Precipitation: All forms of moisture in the atmosphere including rain, hail, sleet and snow.

Quickflow: The surface movement of water, from precipitation, which is not interrupted by vegetation and which runs as a shallow, unchannelled sheet across the soil.

Tributary: A small stream / river which runs into a larger river.

4. Corries, Arêtes, Pyramidal Peaks

- *Corries* are steep-sided hollows in the sides of mountains where snow has accumulated and gradually compacted into ice. The ice in the depression slowly rotated, causing considerable erosion on both the floor and the sides of the hollow. The erosion on the floor was due to abrasion; this led to the floor becoming concave in shape. The erosion also led to the hollow's edge taking on a ridge-shaped appearance. At the sides, plucking of rocks took place as the ice moved forward and the back wall of the depression became very steep.
- As the corrie filled up with ice, eventually it could not contain any more and some of it moved down the slope to a lower level. This was the beginning of a glacier.
- Occasionally as the ice melted, meltwater filled the corrie forming a corrie lake. These are called corrie lochs (Scotland) and tarns (England).
- *Arêtes* – Often corries developed on adjacent sides of a mountain and when they were fully formed they were separated by a 'knife' shaped ridge, termed an arête.
- *Pyramidal Peaks* – If corries develop on all sides of a mountain, the arêtes will form a jagged peak at the top. this feature is called a pyramidal peak. These edges are further sharpened by frost action.

5. Crag and tail, Roche moutonnée

These features occur where the glacier met an outcrop of rock which was harder than the rock of the surrounding area. The sides of the harder rock (crag) are worn away by the glacier but the land behind the crag is protected and forms a long, gently sloping ridge called the tail.

Roche moutonnée are outcrops of harder rocks which have been smoothed on the side facing the ice to give a gentle slope and plucked on the other side to produce a more jagged, steeper slope.

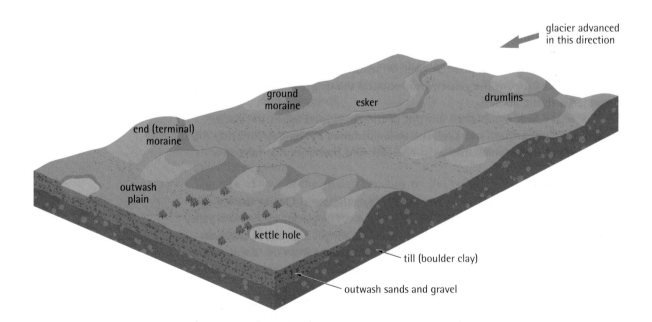

Figure 3·1 (b) – Summary diagram of upland glaciated landscape

Key Point 3

You should be able to label a sketch to show features of glacial erosion and be able to explain how the landscape with these features was formed

Study Figure 3·1 and learn to recognise the various features shown. If asked how the landscape was formed you can refer to the processes of glacial erosion. You may be asked to either annotate the sketch with comments on the formation of individual features or alternatively give a written explanation of how these features were formed.

Features of glacial deposition

1. **Moraines**

   Moraine consists of material known as '*boulder clay*' and '*till*' which has been eroded and transported and deposited by the glacier. This material may be dumped at the end or snout of the glacier and is called 'terminal moraine'. Material dumped at the sides or in the middle of a glacier, where two glaciers came together, are called 'lateral' and 'medial' moraines respectively.

2. **Erratics**

   These are large boulders which have been lifted, carried and deposited by the glaciers some distance away in a different part of the country. The rock type of the erratic is usually different from the rocks which are common to the area in which it is deposited.

3. **Outwash plains**

   These are gently sloping plains consisting of sands and gravel. They have been deposited by meltwater streams flowing out from the ice sheet and carrying material collected by the glacier.

4. **Eskers, Drumlins, Kames**

- *Eskers* are elongated ridges of coarse, stratified, fluvioglacial sands and gravels and are thought to have been formed by meltwater tunnels within the lower parts of the glacier which deposited the material.

- *Drumlins* are oval shaped mounds which can be up to 100 metres high and have a 'basket of eggs' look to them. The material in them was deposited due to friction between the ice and the underlying rock causing the glacier to drop its load.

- *Kames* are irregular shaped mounds of material consisting of sands and gravel, again laid by glacial streams. Sometimes they form terraces on the side of the valley, where the streams ran along the sides of the ice, trapped against it by the valley walls.

Key Point 4

You should be able to use an O.S. map to identify and features of a glaciated landscape and comment on the relief and drainage pattern

On the map you should be able to identify features created by glacial erosion including;

U-shaped valleys, ribbon lakes, corries, corrie lochs / tarns, pyramidal peaks, arêtes, hanging valleys, alluvial fans, misfit streams and truncated spurs.

You should then comment on how the landscape has been affected by this, for instance in terms of the ruggedness of the scenery and the drainage pattern in the area. You could refer to steepness of slopes, the highest and lowest areas and the main drainage systems in the area, noting main rivers and tributaries.

Key Point 5

You should be able to describe how an area has been affected by glacial erosion

These features will also impact on how the land is used for activities such as farming, forestry, communications, settlement, industry and recreational purposes. You could describe the limitations on the use of land for arable farming, the suitability of steep slopes for forestry and the use of U-shaped valleys for communications and settlement.

Key Point 6

You should be able to describe and explain the processes that led to the formation of upland limestone (carboniferous) features.
You should also be able to identify and label the main features of upland limestone areas on maps, sketches and aerial photographs

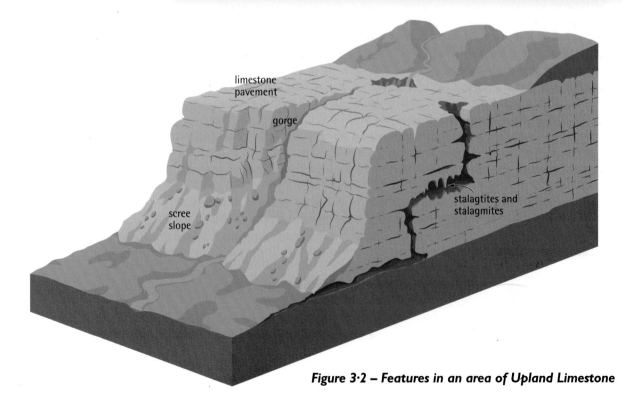

limestone pavement

gorge

scree slope

stalagtites and stalagmites

Figure 3·2 – Features in an area of Upland Limestone

Limestone is a sedimentary rock consisting mainly of calcium carbonate – at least 80%.

Depending on its age it can form several different landforms. Carboniferous limestone was formed about 250 million years ago and its landscapes have specific features which are immediately recognisable including:

1. **Limestone pavements**

   Through glaciers passing over the top of an upland limestone area, the top-soil was removed leaving an area of exposed rock.

   Through the subsequent chemical action of rainwater dissolving the limestone, joints widened and deepened on the surface creating large blocks resembling pavements.

   The cracks or fissures between the blocks are called grykes and the large blocks separated by the grykes are called clints.

   Pot holes / swallow holes are formed where persistent widening of a major joint occured, possibly by a stream disappearing underground.

2. **Intermittent drainage**

   Intermittent drainage occurs on limestone areas when streams which drain areas of impermeable rock carry on into the limestone area and disappear through the permeable limestone thus interrupting the course of the stream.

3. **Underground caverns**

   As the process of dissolving the limestone continues, underground sections of the rock may collapse onto the bedrock creating underground caves. As the surface water meets the impermeable underground rock, this can lead to the creation of underground lakes and streams.

4. **Stalagmites and Stalactites**

   Stalactites and Stalagmites are formed underground in caverns. These are deposits of the mineral calcite that either hang down from the ceiling of the cave (stalactites), or deposits that build up from the ground (stalagmites).

5. **Scarp slopes**

   The edge of the limestone area which is exposed to the elements can form a steep slope known as a scar or scarp slope through the process of frost shattering whereby water seeps into little cracks on the slope surface and freezes during cold winters.

   Areas of upland limestone in Britain form a rolling plateau-like landscape which has limited surface drainage.

   Due to the lack of water, vegetation is sparse or non-existent. Exposed hard grey limestone is clearly seen on the surface. This landscape is referred to as karst scenery.

Coastal landforms

Key Point 7

You should be able to identify certain coastal landforms and explain how they were formed including: cliffs, wave-cut platforms, caves, arches, stacks, headlands, bays, spits, bars, longshore drift

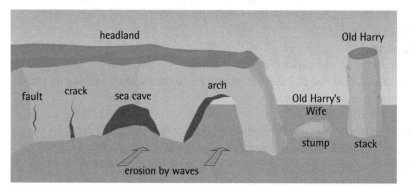

Figure 3·3 – A typical landscape of headlands, caves, arches and stacks

Formation of coastal features

Cliffs, wave-cut platforms, headlands and bays
* *Cliffs* are formed by wave action undercutting land which meets the sea. This occurs at about high tide level. A notch is cut and, as the land recedes, the cliff base is deepened by wave erosion. At the same time the cliff face is continually attacked by weathering processes. Mass wasting such as slumping occurs, causing the cliff face to become less steep.
* When steep waves break at the bottom of a cliff, the cliff is undercut forming a feature called a 'wave-cut notch'. Continual undercutting causes the cliff to eventually collapse and, as this process is repeated, the cliff retreats leaving a gently sloping wave-cut platform. The slope angle of this is less than 4°.
* When resistant rocks alternate with less resistant rocks along a coastline and all are under constant wave attack, the resistant rocks form *headlands* whilst the bands of less resistant rock are worn away to form *bays*.
* Bays and headlands can also develop in a single rock structure, e.g. limestone which has lines of weakness such as joints or faults.
* Although the headlands gradually become more vulnerable to erosion nevertheless they protect the adjacent bays from from the effects of destructive waves.

Caves, arches and stacks
* *Caves* are formed when waves attack cliffs with resistant rock along lines of weakness such as faults and joints.
* The waves undercut part of the cliff and can cut right through the cave to form an *arch*. Continual erosion causes the arch to widen and eventually the roof of the arch collapses to leave a piece rock left standing called a *stack*.

Spits and bars

- *Spits* result from marine deposition. They consist of a long narrow accumulation of sand or shingle with one part still attached to the land.
- The other end projects at a narrow angle into the sea or across an estuary. This end is often hooked or curved. Spurn Head on the Humber estuary is a good example of a spit.
- *Bars* are ridges of sediment formed parallel to the coast and can be exposed at high or low tides.
- *Tombolos*: Often bars form barriers across bays. If a bar joins an island to the mainland it is called a tombolo. A very well known example of a tombolo in Britain is Chesil Beach near Weymouth in Dorset.

Longshore drift

Longshore drift is the process by which waves carry material up and down a beach. This material is usually deposited in a zig zag fashion due to the effects of winds on waves.

To prevent the movement of beach material away from beaches by longshore drift, wooden or stone walls called 'groynes' are built along beaches.

Although groynes protect some parts of beaches, areas on either side are often depleted of sand.

> **Key Point 8**
>
> **You should be able to describe and explain the processes involved in the modification of coastal landforms including attrition, corrasion, hydraulic action, longshore drift, sea level changes, slumping, rockfalls and cliff-line retreat**

The processes include:

- *Corrasion* (abrasion) is caused by waves throwing beach material against cliffs.
- *Attrition* happens when waves cause rocks and boulders to break up into small particles by the bumping them together.
- *Hydraulic action* is the process of waves compressing air in cracks in cliffs. As a result, any weaknesses in the rockface of cliffs and headlands are widened creating caves.
- *Longshore drift* occurs when waves remove material from beaches and deposit this material further down the coast.
- *Sea level changes* happened in post-glacial periods when large amounts of ice melted and caused sea levels to rise, often drowning parts of coastlines.
- *Slumping* is the movement of surface rocks or superficial material which has become detached from a hillside or cliff face.
- *Rockfalls* occur when small blocks of rock become detached from a cliff face due to the sea undercutting the cliff along joint patterns.
- *Cliff-line retreat* happens when the cliff face is gradually worn back by slumping, undercutting and rockfalls.

Key Point 9

You should know about the effects of sea level changes on coastlines

These are due to and include points such as:
- During the ice age vast amounts of water were locked up as ice and snow. This caused sea levels throughout the world to fall.
- When the ice melted sea levels rose, often drowning many coastal areas.
- Valleys formed either by rivers or by glaciers which met the sea were drowned to form landscape features called *rias* and *fjords*.
- *Rias* formed from drowned river valleys have relatively low, gentle sides making them ideal for harbours.
- *Fjords* result from a rise in seal level which drowns valleys which were overdeepened by glaciers. They are long and narrow and are shallow at the entrance. This may be due to deposits of moraine left by the glacier at the entrance. Consequently they are less suited to major harbour development.
- Good examples of rias are found in south west England and south west Ireland whilst north west Scotland and the coastline of Norway feature excellent examples of fjords.

Key Point 10

You should be able to identify the features of a glaciated landscape, upland limestone landscape and coastal features

The following examples give an indication of what the features will look like on an O.S. map. Study these and try to identify similar patterns on different map extracts.

As well as identifying the features from the maps, you will probably also be required to name examples of these features and to provide appropriate six figure grid references.

Key Point 11

You should be able to use an O.S. map to provide evidence of change due to weathering and erosion

- You may be able to describe erosion due to the effect of glaciers or rivers by referring to specific features or stages of river development.
- Refer to evidence of mechanical weathering by noting the presence of scree on particular slopes, indicating the effect of freeze-thaw action.

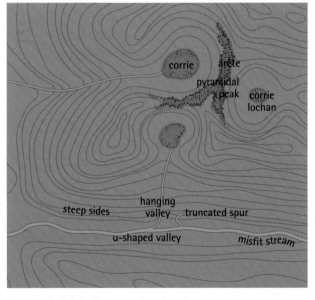

Figure 3·4 (a) Glaciated uplands

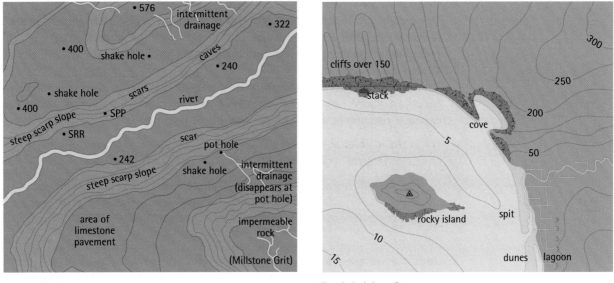

Fig 3·2 (b) – Upland Limestone

Fig 3·2 (c) – Coasts

- If the area on the map shows an area of upland limestone, you may refer to the impact of chemical weathering by noting the occurrence of limestone pavement, swallow holes and pot holes and caverns.
- Note the lack of surface vegetation in a limestone area and refer to the impact of glaciers in removing the original vegetation.
- In a coastal area you may refer to cliffs, headlands, stacks, caves and bays.

Processes of slope formation

Key Point 12

You should be able to describe and explain the processes of weathering and erosion which have led to the formation of physical features in the landscape

Weathering involves the natural breaking down of rocks into smaller particles. There are basically three types of weathering: physical, biological and chemical weathering.

1. **Physical weathering**

   This involves the disintegration of rocks into smaller particles without altering their chemical composition. This can involves processes such as:

   Exfoliation – with extreme daily changes in temperature, rocks can expand and contract. Gradually this weakens the rock until the outer layer eventually breaks away from the rest of the rock. Sometimes this process is referred to as 'onion weathering'.

   Frost shattering – water which seeps into small cracks or fissures in rocks can freeze during sub-zero temperatures. As the temperature rises between 0 and 4°C the ice expands and exerts pressure on the rock. Gradually pieces of rock break off and may fall down slopes, collecting at the bottom as scree.

2. **Biological weathering**
   This includes root action or burrowing. Tree roots can disturb rocks and break them open as they spread. Animals burrowing into the soil can also expose rocks and cause them to widen and break down.
3. **Chemical weathering**
   Rainwater, or water which seeps through vegetation such as moorland, can become acidic. When this water comes into contact with rocks it can result in a chemical reaction in which the rock begins to break down.

Key Point 13

You should be able to describe and explain the conditions and processes which have led to the formation of rockfall, scree slopes and landslip especially as these affect coastlines

These processes are referred to as mass movements. However in the new syllabus you will not be expected to answer a question on the general topic of 'mass movement'. But it is important to have some knowledge of them since they affect other landscapes including areas of upland glaciation, upland limestone and coasts. Particles of rock are removed by processes such as soil creep, mud flows, rock falls and landslips / landslides. These processes contribute to the formation of slopes. Mass movement of soil and rocks can range from minimal, almost imperceptible, movement such as soil creep to dramatic movements such as landslides.

Factors influencing movements include
1. **The degree of slope**
   Slopes which are gentle (no more than 5°) are more likely to experience soil creep whereby the soil gradually and slowly moves down the slope. Steeper, almost vertical slopes will often have rock falls due to weathering (especially freeze-thaw action) and debris called scree will gather near the bottom part of the slope.
2. **Water content**
   If the water content of the soil increases (for example during periods of heavy rainfall) the soil becomes saturated and may begin to move or slip over the bottom layers. This can lead to mud and earth flows. These types of flows are rapid.
3. **Nature of underlying rock**
   There are occasions where strong rocks are underlain by relatively weaker rock strata. If the underlying strata is worn away it will be unable to support the rocks above it and this can result in landslides or slumping.

Key Point 14

You should be able to describe and explain the conditions and processes which have led to the formation of landslips / landslides and rockfall / scree

1. **Land slips / Landslides**

   This kind of movement often occurs in areas where the underlying rock is softer than the rock above. Erosion of the underlying rock by rivers or sea action will undercut the rock causing violent, sudden falls of the overlying rock.

2. **Rockfall / Scree**

   This is a rapid process which occurs on steep slopes. Water entering cracks in the rocks freezes during cold spells. The expansion of the freezing water widens the cracks and fragments of rock break off. These fall down slope under gravity and collect at the bottom of the slope as scree.

GEOGRAPHICAL METHODS AND TECHNIQUES

Key Point 15

You should be able to use an O.S. map to describe and account for the relief of an area and the influence of physical factors on the drainage pattern

- When presented with an O.S. map, you should divide the map into areas where the relief is similar (for example main valleys, areas of upland or highland).
- You could show these areas on a sketch, labelling each area accordingly.
- You should then describe the relief of each of these areas in turn, noting factors such as steepness of slopes and gradients, spot heights, the amount of area covered, as well as specific features (rivers, streams, confluence points, meanders, tributaries and hills).
- Note any physical factors which may affect drainage such as type of rock (permeable or impermeable), the presence of clay (which is usually indicated by bog or marshland) the stage of development of rivers (young, mature or old).
- Note features within the drainage pattern such as meanders, ox-bow lakes, direction of flow, gradients, tidal limits and estuaries.

Key Point 16

You should be able to identify and annotate landscape features on a diagram

The diagram may refer to any of the landscape types already discussed. In examination questions you may also be asked to explain the formation of these features and perhaps include relevant explanatory points on the diagram.

Key Point 17

You should be able to construct and interpret cross-sections and transects

Although you will not be asked to construct a cross-section in the external exam, you could be asked to identify certain features on a cross-section from a map of a glaciated upland area or an area of upland limestone.

SAMPLE QUESTIONS, ANSWERS, COMMENTS AND MARKING INSTRUCTIONS

Question 1

(a) Study the OS map extract number 1056/OLM2: Ingleton
The area of the Yorkshire Dales National Park, shown on the map, is characterised by Upland Limestone scenery.
Describe the evidence to support the above statement, referring to specific named features shown on the map extract.
6 marks

(b) Choose any one Upland Limestone feature (other than waterfalls), described in your answer to part (a), and, with the aid of a diagram, explain its formation.
3 marks

Sample answer – 1(a)
✓ **denotes a correct point**

> Limestone scenery can be found in Twistleton Scars ✓ 715764. Shake holes ✓ and pot holes where there are fissures in the limestone can be found in Rantry Hole 722732 ✓ and Gritstone Pot 726731.
> Disappearing stream can be found at 744723 ✓ where water comes off the impervious cap rock and disappears down fissures in the limestone ✓.
> Limestone pavement ✓ can be found at Green Edge 729744 ✓.

Comments and marks obtained – 1(a)
The first paragraph has references to four correct features with appropriate grid references and would be worth $4 \times \frac{1}{2}$ marks. The references to the 'disappearing streams', limestone pavements and the location at Green Edge would merit a further $3 \times \frac{1}{2}$ marks.
The correct grid references would gain a further $2 \times \frac{1}{2}$ marks giving a total of $4\frac{1}{2}$ marks out of a possible 6 marks.
Reference to other surface limestone features would have gained additional marks, but these were not given in the answer. An above average answer.

OS map extract number 1056/OLM2: Ingleton

Reproduced from Ordnance Survey mapping on behalf of the controller of Her Majesty's Stationery Office © Crown copyright 2004. 100036009

Sample answer – 1(b)

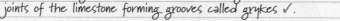
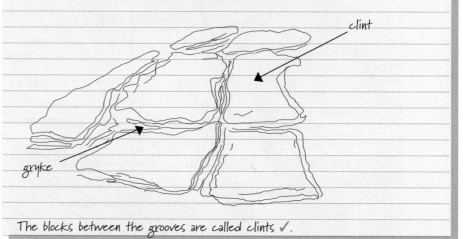

Limestone pavement is formed when glacier ice strips ✓ away the overlying topsoil leaving the underlying limestone bare ✓.
Rainwater, being a weak carbonic acid ✓ begins to weather ✓ away the joints of the limestone forming grooves called grykes ✓.

clint

gryke

The blocks between the grooves are called clints ✓.

Comments and marks obtained – 1(b)

The candidate correctly indicates the work of the glacier in the formation process and 'leaving the underlying limestone bare', are sufficient for $2 \times \frac{1}{2}$ marks.

The further statements on the chemical erosion of the limestone through 'weak carbonic acid in rainwater' and the correct identification of the joints and blocks – grykes and clints – would merit a further $3 \times \frac{1}{2}$ marks with a final $\frac{1}{2}$ mark for the diagram.

This would result in a total of 3 marks out of the possible 4 marks available. A solid pass.

Question 2

(a) Describe the evidence which shows that the Great Langdale Valley has been affected by processes of glacial erosion.
5 marks

(b) Explain, with the aid of a diagram, the formation of either
(i)   a corrie or
(ii)   a hanging valley
4 marks

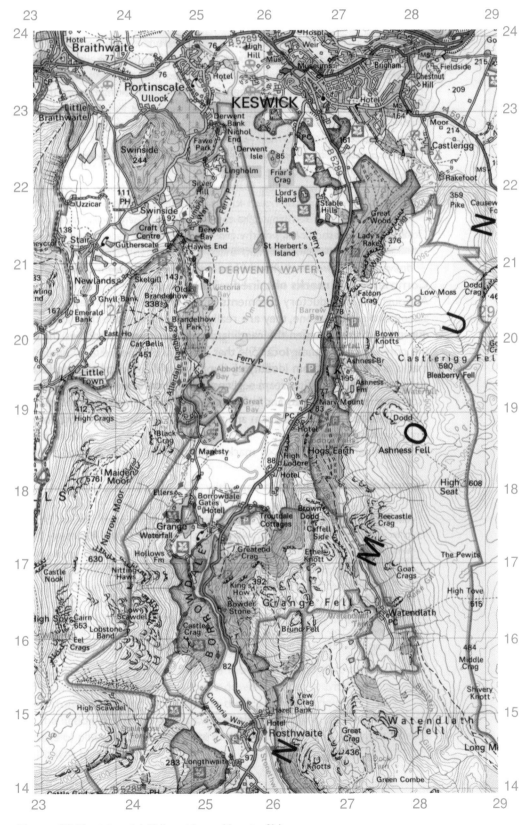

Reference Diagram Q3 (Great Langdale Valley – plan and long profile)

Reproduced from Ordnance Survey mapping on behalf of the controller of Her Majesty's Stationery Office © Crown copyright 2004. 100036009

7. Two other processes are important namely eluviation and illuviation. *Eluviation* means the washing out of material, i.e. the removal of elements such as calcium and aluminium, and organic material from the A horizon. *Illuviation* means the deposition of this washed material in the subsoil. Heavy, minerals are deposited much deeper and this obviously affects the fertility of the soil.

8. Organisms within the soil affect the breakdown and decay of vegetation and therefore impact on the depth of the humus layer. Any living creatures such as insects and worms also affect the development of the soil since they can expose the soil to air and can add to the chemical balance of the soil through their excreta.

9. In areas with cool climates with mainly coniferous forest, and where precipitation greatly exceeds evapotranspiration, a process known as *podzolisation* is common. Percolating rainwater becomes quite acidic as it passes through an acidic humus formed from fallen pine cones and needles.
   This water dissolves and removes iron and aluminium oxides from the topsoil, leaving behind a high level of silica in the A horizon which is bleached and drained of coloured minerals.

10. When waterlogged conditions exist in the soil (if the subsoil is full of stagnating water which loses oxygen) a process known as *gleying* occurs. This often happens in poorly drained areas where the land is more gently sloping.

Key Point 3
You should able to recognise and describe the properties of soils from a soil profile

Soil Types

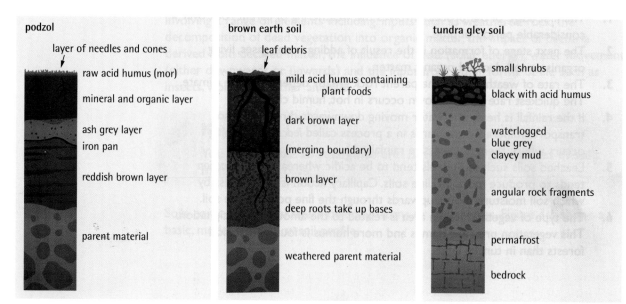

Figure 4·2 – Selected soil profiles (podzols, brown earth, tundra)

Podzols – soil properties

- These soils are found in a wide belt across the northern hemisphere, particularly in the areas of *taiga* or coniferous forests. Fallen pine needles and cones create an acidic humus called mor. The soil has well defined layers since there is very little movement and mixing of the horizons due to the absence of earth worms because of the cold conditions.
- The upper A horizon has an ash grey colour due to the removal of the minerals.
- With aluminium and iron oxides concentrating in the B horizon, a cementing effect takes place between the A and B horizons, forming a *hardpan* which seriously affects the drainage through the soil. This results in the upper layers becoming waterlogged.
- The B horizon is reddish brown in colour from the iron oxides.
- The subsoil consists of weathered parent rock.
- Decomposition of the Ao horizon is very slow due to the cold climatic conditions. In addition to moderate precipitation, meltwater released from snow or ice during the spring produces leaching of iron and aluminium oxides from the A horizon leaving a high silica residue.

Gley / tundra – soil properties

- The subsoil in tundra areas remain frozen throughout year. During the brief summer the ground surface thaws but the melt water cannot drain freely due to the frozen subsoil or permafrost layer. This results in the soil becoming waterlogged or *gleyed*.
- Bacterial action is very restricted due to the cold temperatures. The waterlogged soil lacks oxygen and the tundra vegetation is also very limited.
  - Alternate periods of freezing and thawing cause great disturbance and mixing of the soil.
  - Consequently the horizons are less well defined.
  - The A horizon contains black, acidic humus only partially decayed due to low temperatures.
  - The B horizon is bluish grey in colour with clayey mud.
- Fragments of weathered parent material are often found within the B horizon.
- The cold conditions of the climate severely restrict the use of these soils.

Brown earth soils – soil properties

- These soils are associated with areas of deciduous forest. They are sometimes referred to as *alfisols*. The humus layer is thick and generally fertile due to the variety of vegetation which is decayed. With warmer conditions the leaf litter which accumulates in autumn decomposes quickly due to organisms in the soil. The humus is less acidic and is referred to as *mull*.
- Precipitation exceeds evaporation sufficiently to cause leaching. However there is not enough to cause podzolisation. There is an absence of bases especially calcium and magnesium in the A horizon.
- The horizons merge more than the podzols due to the activity of earthworms and insects (biota).
- With the redeposition of iron and aluminium due to illuviation, the colour of the soil becomes increasingly reddish brown.
- Unlike podzols there is no hardpan and so the soils tend to be free-draining.
- There is a high clay content throughout the profile of brown earth soils and this increases the fertility of the soil although lime is often added to improve fertility even further.

GEOGRAPHICAL METHODS AND TECHNIQUES

Key Point 4

You should be able to describe and analyse soil profiles, particularly those of podzols, brown earth and gley / tundra profiles

Analysis:
*   You should begin your analysis by noting the various constituents of the different horizons within the profile, beginning with the topsoil.
*   Describe the thickness of this layer and refer to reasons for this, for example depth of humus layer and vegetation.
*   Each layer would then be discussed in turn with reference to thickness, content, colour, texture, water content and whether the layers of the A, B and C horizons are well-defined or whether mixing has occurred.
*   The properties of the horizons may be explained by reference to factors such as climate, vegetation, processes of leaching, eluviation and illuviation and soil biota.
*   From this description and explanation you should be able to deduce the type of soil which the given soil profile shows.

Vegetation

Key Point 5

You should be able to explain the term 'ecosystem' and the processes which produce ecosystems on various scales for example from a pond to a forest area

An ecosystem is the system in which plants, animals, insects and micro-organisms interact with the natural environment which includes climate, rocks and soils. Ecosystems can vary in size from very small pieces of land in the corner of a garden, to ponds or areas of bog or wetlands to whole zones of desert areas or rainforest.

Processes:
All ecosystems depend on two basic processes:
*   Flow of energy, the main source of which is the sun. This solar energy is absorbed by plants and converted into chemical energy (food) by photosynthesis. This chemical energy passes through the ecosystem in food chains. Each node (species) in the chain depends on the preceding nodes for food and energy.
*   Recycling of nutrients in which some nutrients are continually recycled within the ecosystem. Plants absorb nutrients form the soil and these are passed on to animals which eat plants. When plants and animals die, they eventually decay and decompose and the nutrients within them are returned to the soil.

The vegetation within any given area can be considered as a community of plant life. Certain plants may be favoured by changing environmental conditions and this leads to a process of community change known as plant succession

Key Point 6

You should be able to explain fully what is meant by the term 'climax vegetation'

Climax vegetation is the final stage in the process known as plant succession. Climate is regarded as the principal factor in the climax vegetation of a region and therefore the final stage is called the climatic climax vegetation.

Key Point 7

You should be able to describe an explain the process known as 'plant succession'

The process of plant succession involves a series of stages during which the species of plant life changes. this whole process from the initial establishment, the pioneer stage, of vegetation to the final stage or climax is called a sere.

These stages of plant succession are sometimes termed seral succession.

- The first of these stages is referred to as the *pioneer stage* or *prisere*. At this stage the first plants that colonise a completely new, perhaps bare site such as a beach or sand dune, are called *pioneers*.
- The pioneer plants, through their root action, begin to bind the soil together preventing its removal by wind or rain. Gradually the soil is protected and this assists in the process of plant succession.
- The pioneer plants add organic matter to the soil that holds water and nutrients. This in turn changes the conditions of the site sufficiently so as to allow other less resilient plants to become established.
- Lichens and mosses which were present in the pioneer stage may be replaced by grasses which in turn may eventually give way to shrubs and woodland.

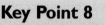

Key Point 8

You should be able to describe and explain plant succession to be found across a sand dune transect, referring to the names of specific plants

Vegetation succession on Coastal Dune Area

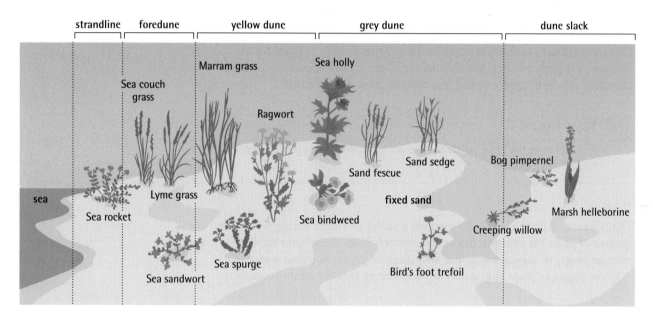

Figure 4·3 – Plant succession on dune belt (psammosere)

Description and explanation might include points such as:

- Dunes are formed from sediments deposited along the sea shore which have been blown inland. The first dunes to develop are known as embryo dunes. These are the youngest and most scattered of the dune system. Some species which can tolerate the harsh conditions include couch grass, marram grass and ragwort.
- The embryo dunes are succeeded by 'yellow' dunes, so-called because of the yellow colour of the large amount of bare sand. These pioneering species allow weathering to begin and for succession to occur further inland.
- Mosses and lichens begin to colonise the dunes and in time create the conditions for further species to develop, especially those which tolerate alkaline conditions.
- As the dunes begin to stabilise, humus accumulates from decaying marram grass and soil forms on the surface.
- In time, more mature vegetation forms on the older dunes including woodland with pine, holly and oaks further inland.
- Grassland is found in areas with a high proportion of calcium carbonate from shell fragments whereas heath is more likely to develop on more acidic soils.
- Between the dunes are damp hollow areas where water gathers called slacks. Plant life in these areas includes marsh plants, rushes, alder and small willow trees.

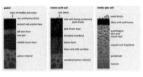

Reference Diagram Q1

SAMPLE QUESTIONS, ANSWERS, COMMENTS AND MARKING INSTRUCTIONS

Question 1

(a)   Study Reference Diagram Q1 (see Figure 4·2 on page 76)
Choose one of the following soil types:
(i) podzol (ii) brown earth (iii) gley,
and describe the influence of the various soil forming factors on its formation.
5 marks

(b)   Explain fully what is meant by the term 'climax vegetation'.
3 marks

Sample answer – 1(a)
✓ denotes correct point

acidic humus
coniferous trees leaching Fe and Al oxides
shallow roots B horizon
Iron pan   ✓
C horizon
Parent material   ✓

In areas where the podzol soil is found the climate is cold and wet ✓ which is the ideal conditions for coniferous trees, which have shallow roots and can't bring nutrients up through the soil. This makes the needles and cones which fall off the tree acidic ✓, which also makes the humus acidic with a P.H. of 4 – 5.5 ✓ Also because of the cold climate there are few organisms which means there is little mixing and the horizons are clearly seen. There also won't be a lot of decomposition as there are few organisms ✓ which means there are less nutrients in the soil. Due to the wet climate ✓ and the shallow roots not being able to bind the soil there is a lot of leaching of Fe and Al oxides ✓ which form an iron pan which also stops nutrients from being brought up ✓. With packed soil usually being found on steep slopes this promotes leaching and podsolisation of the minerals and nutrients.

Comments and marks obtained – 1(*a*)

The answer begins with an appropriate diagram which refers to vegetation, processes and the soil profile. The diagram would probably obtain $2 \times \frac{1}{2}$ marks. The next reference to climate is worth a further   mark and the comments on the acidity of the pine needles giving a pH of $4 \cdot 5 - 5 \cdot 5$ would gain a further $2 \times \frac{1}{2}$ marks.

The correct references to lack of organisms and leaching of Fe and Al oxides forming a hard pan due to the wet climate would merit a further $4 \times \frac{1}{2}$ marks. The final statement repeats earlier references already credited.

The total marks obtained therefore would be $4\frac{1}{2}$ out of 5 for this answer. A good answer.

Sample answer – 1(*b*)

> Climax vegetation is the final stage ✓ in plant succession ✓, where the ecosystem is at equilibrium ✓ and the biomass is at a maximum ✓. There are no more big changes. There are large trees found at this stage like oak. ✓

Comments and marks obtained – 1(*b*)

There are several important points mentioned in the answer which clearly illustrate a good understanding of the term 'climax vegetation'. The candidate notes that this is the 'final stage' in 'plant succession' and that the 'ecosystem is in equilibrium' and 'biomass is at a maximum'.

Types of vegetation are correctly identified including 'oak'. These points would merit $\frac{1}{2}$ mark each giving a total of $2\frac{1}{2}$ marks. Some further elaboration of the terms 'equilibrium' or 'biomass' would probably have earned a further $\frac{1}{2}$ mark. The answer gains a total of 7 marks out of a possible 8 for parts (*a*) and (*b*).

Question 2

(*a*)   Study Reference Diagram Q2A. (See Figure 4·3 on page 80) Describe and explain the changes in the type of plants to be found across the sand dune transect.

6 marks

Reference Diagram Q2A

Sample answer – 2 (a)

As you move inland there is increased vegetation ✓, humus content and moisture. The reason behind this is the area nearest to the sea (embryo dunes) has very little humus ✓, nutrients and moisture content. Very little vegetation can grow here. Only xerophytic plants can survive here, these are plants that can survive any harsh and poor conditions ✓.

Species like marram grass can survive here because they can get their adequate nutrients from the rain ✓ itself. When these plants die and decay ✓ into the dune, this places nutrients and some humus into the soil ✓, therefore different species can adapt to these areas. Moving further inland more and more species are found because there is more humic content which means more fertile ground which enables more species. At the climax stage, the ground is at very good climatic and ground conditions therefore the larger more dominating varieties ✓ of plant grow there ie, deciduous trees like oak and ash ✓. Some species may disappear due to competition with the larger more dominating species ✓ for food and light.

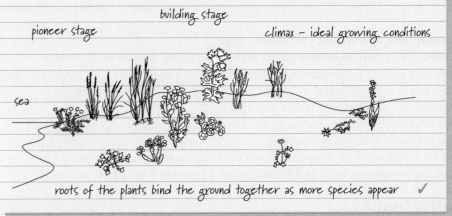

pioneer stage

building stage

climax – ideal growing conditions

sea

roots of the plants bind the ground together as more species appear ✓

Comments and marks obtained – 2(a)

The first two statements relating to increased vegetation further inland and the embryo dunes having very little humus would probably be worth $2 \times \frac{1}{2}$ marks. The explanation about the types of plant which can survive would gain a further $\frac{1}{2}$ mark although the reference to marram grass is perhaps a little premature and confused.

Comments on the dying and decaying and consequent addition of nutrient and humus to the soil giving rise to a wider range of species of plant would be worth an additional $2 \times \frac{1}{2}$ marks.

There is some repetition in this part of the answer which would not be credited.

The reference to larger, more dominant species at the climax stage, the identification of types of plant, oak (deciduous trees) and the disappearance of other species due to competition would complete the marks obtained by gaining a final $4 \times \frac{1}{2}$ marks. The lack of reference to the psammosere and actual types of plant life at different stages possibly limits the total number of marks obtained.

The total number of marks obtained therefore would be $4\frac{1}{2}$ out of 6. A good answer.

Marking instructions

Question 1

1(a) Assess out of 5 – each relevant point gains $\frac{1}{2}$ mark

Maximum of 4 if no diagram.

Fully annotated diagrams could gain the maximum 5 marks available.

To obtain full marks candidates would be expected to recognise the part played by all soil forming factors. The relative importance of each factor would depend on the soil type chosen for discussion.

For **podzol**, candidates might suggest:

- Dark, raw acidic (mor) humus due to the natural vegetation cover of pine needles and fir cones. Plant litter breaks down slowly because of the cold climate. There is heavy leaching of iron and aluminium oxides from the topsoil (eluviation) due to the excess of precipitation over evaporation and by spring snow melt.
- These oxides are deposited in the subsoil or B horizon (illuviation) forming a hard pan, which in turn impedes drainage. This causes waterlogging in the topsoil. This is what produces the red-brown colouring.
- The soil horizons are clearly defined because the cold climate severely restricts the impact of soil biota in helping to mix material between the horizons.

For **gley** soil:

- Drainage is a key factor. There is a high water content and lack of oxygen in soil spaces. Soils are damp and waterlogged because of inadequate drainage due to permafrost layer lying a short distance below surface.
- Horizons are poorly defined; this is due to the constant freezing and thawing leading to contractions and expansions which causes vertical mixing within the soil.
- Some weathered particles of parent material are obvious within the blue / grey and peaty clays of the B horizon. Humus consists of mainly dark acid (mor) derived from natural vegetation of mosses and lichens.
- There is little bacterial action due to waterlogging which causes oxygen deficiency, and the cold winter temperatures and short, mild summer. As a result, the decay of the humus layer is a very slow process.

For **brown earth** soil:

- There is moderate leaching since precipitation generally exceeds evaporation. In some areas where there is more active leaching, iron pans may develop.
- With the milder climate, plant materials decompose more quickly than in podzols. There is much more biotic activity, both in terms of bacterial activity and in the action of earthworms, insects and rodents.
- Thus there is more mixing between the horizons. There is a plentiful supply of plant litter from mostly deciduous trees.
- Humus layer is thicker and only slightly acidic. This improves availability of plant nutrients for vegetation.

1 (b) Assess out of 3 – each relevant point gains $\frac{1}{2}$ mark.
Climax vegetation is the final stage in the development of the natural vegetation in any given locale or region. When this happens, the composition of the plant community is relatively stable and in equilibrium with the existing environmental conditions.

This state is normally determined by climate and or soil.

Candidates should be able to show knowledge of the evolution of plant life from the early colonisation stage by pioneer species, through succession to climax vegetation.

Question 2.

2 (a) Assess out of 5 or 6 with each relevant point being awarded a $\frac{1}{2}$ mark.
For full credit all stages of the psammosere must be included.

Answers that simply relate information from the table to parts of the dune system without mentioning plants by name should receive a maximum of 4 marks.

Answers which simply describe plant distributions would obtain only a maximum of 2.

The following plants and conditions may be referred to at various stages across the psammosere.

- **Embryo dunes** – sea twitch; lyme grass; sea couch – all of these plants can withstand the desiccating effect of the sand as well as the high salt content / alkalinity and lack of humus.
- The decay of these plants helps to produce limited humus for the next stage.
- **Fore dune** – sea twitch; marram grass. Salt content decreases although it is still fairly alkaline.
- Humus content increases slightly. Marram grass can begin to grow and this helps to stabilise the sand dunes. As the sand builds up, roots of marram help to bind the soil.
- **Main dune** – marram grass.
- Alkalinity decreasing and acidity increasing slightly inland.
- Greater amount of humus from decay of vegetation on the fore-dune – marram fully developed.
- **Older dune ridge**: marram grass; red fescue; sea spurge; small herbs / heather.
- Soil becoming increasingly acid with the greater humus content and more sheltered, less salty environment permitting a wider range of plants to exist. Then gorse; bracken; ragwort heather plants also have access to the water table and in the slacks where water accumulates.
- Plants such as creeping willow, cotton grass and reeds exist followed by small trees; pine, birch, alder; large trees – oak, ash.
- Moving towards climax, the conditions with greater humus content and greater shelter, providing better conditions for plant growth.

The Human Environment

POPULATION

DEMOGRAPHIC SYSTEMS AND POPULATION CHANGE

Key Point 1

You should be able to interpret population pyramids for Economically More Developed Countries (EMDCs or developed countries) and Economically Less Developed Countries (ELDCs or developing countries) and account for the different structures

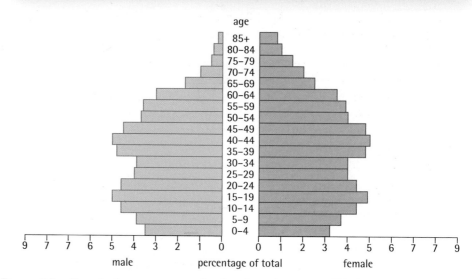

Figure 5·1 – Population structure of a developed country (EMDC)

This structure indicates a developed country. Its main features include:
- A fairly low birth rate in both males and females
- A bulge in the middle age groups, e.g. 15–60 indicating that most of the population are within this range.
- A fairly high percentage of the population within the upper age groups from 60+. This indicates that the country has a high life expectancy and also an ageing population.
- All of these features indicate a developed country but the structure has consequences for the country in terms of its social and economic development.

Reasons for structure

Reasons include the overall wealth of the country and the high standard of living enjoyed by its population. Standards of healthcare, education, housing, employment are all high. Average income per head of population is also high. The number of children per family is usually low due to factors including the widespread use of contraception and couples having children much later in marriage. Life expectancy is high and this accounts for the fairly high percentages in the age groups 60+.

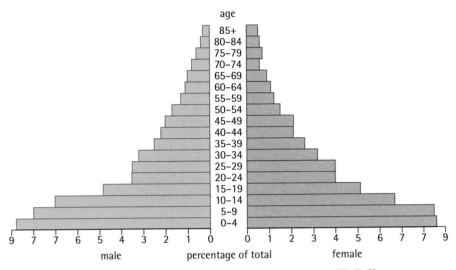

Figure 5·2 – Population structure of a developing country (ELDC)

This structure indicates a developing country. Its main features include:
- A high birth rate for both males and females.
- A large proportion of the population between the ages of 0–15 years.
- A more definite pyramidal shape where the numbers of people in the upper age groups above 15 years decreases fairly rapidly.
- Very few people in the higher age groups above 60+ years (i.e. a country where the average life expectancy is quite low).

Reasons for structure
The reasons for this structure are related to the overall lack of development in all areas of the country for example in terms of wealth, industrial growth, health, education, food supply and general quality of life.
Lack of economic prosperity is usually the main cause of these problems.

Key Point 2
You should understand various terms relating to demographic trends

These include:
(Crude Birth Rate) – C.B.R.
This figure indicates the number of people per thousand head of population, born in any given year. Since this is the basic measure it is termed 'crude'.
(Crude Death Rate / Crude Mortality Rate) C.D.R.
This indicates the number of people per thousand of population who die in any given year.
Natural Growth Rate
Subtracting death rates from birth rates gives a basic indication of the number by which the population is increasing each year per thousand head of the population.

Average Life Expectancy

This is a figure which indicates the average number of years a person can expect to live within any given country, e.g. male 67 years, female 70 years.

(Infant Mortality rate) – I.M.R.

This rate indicates the number of deaths of infants under one year of age per thousand live births in any given year.

> ### Key Point 3
>
> **You must be able to describe and explain population structures and also describe and give reasons for any changes which may have taken place in populations of certain parts of the world**

Population structure

- The structure of the population of a given country is defined in terms of age and sex distribution. Age is divided into different age groups, e.g. 0–4, 5–9 and so on. Data on these characteristics are plotted on a graph called a population pyramid (see Figures 5·1 and 5·2) and is based on grouping males and females into different age groups from 0 to 80+.

- Variations in birth rates, death rates, and the movement of people into and out of a country on a permanent basis (migration patterns), have a direct impact on the structure of the population of any given country.

- Structures can show variations in levels of development, imbalances in the population, changes in the population due to factors such as wars and migration; they also suggest problems which specific countries may be facing in relation to their populations.

- Analysis of population structure graphs (age / sex pyramids) reveals patterns of birth and death rates and an estimation of the life expectancy in general terms.

- In the first graph (Figure 5·1), the birth rate is fairly low as is the death rate. People will tend to have a fairly high life expectancy as the number of people of both sexes in the groups beyond 60+ is a relatively high proportion of the rest of the population shown on the graph.

- The structure is fairly well balanced in that the number of males and females is evenly distributed throughout the different age groups.

- The shape of the pyramid shows a very gradual tapering off towards the upper age groups.

- There is no imbalance between the lower groups between 0–15 and the groups between 15–60. In effect the base is neither significantly wider – indicating a high birth rate, or significantly narrower – indicating quite a low birth rate.

- The very gradual narrowing of the groups towards the upper end indicates quite a low death rate in both males and females.

- The first graph is typical of a developed world country.

- The second graph (Figure 5·2) has a wide base for both males and females up to the 10–14 age group which indicates a high birth rate, typical of a developing country.

- The middle part of the graph becomes narrower and the upper part in the 50–60+ age groups becomes very narrow suggesting a low life expectancy rate. Again this is typical of a developing country.

Key Point 4

With reference to population structures, you should be able to discuss the problems that might arise from a rise in birth and death rates in developing countries and a fall in birth rates in developed countries

Consequences of **rising birth rates** and **falling death rates** in developing countries include:

- *Overpopulation*, which is said to exist whenever a reduction in the existing population would result in an improvement in the quality of life for the remaining population.
- A *lack of sufficient food* to meet demand due to the inability of the country to provide the amount needed.
- *Inadequate housing* for the population, particularly in cities and towns. This severely reduces the quality of life for a large proportion of the population. Vast numbers of people in developing countries are forced to live in very poor accommodation such as shanty towns.
- These areas often lack the basic facilities of sewage, electricity and water supply. As a result water-borne diseases such as typhoid are widespread.
- *High levels of unemployment* occur since there are far too many people for the jobs available.
- As a result there will be widespread poverty. This is made worse by the lack of government financial aid.
- *Lack of services* (such as health centres, hospitals, doctors, schools and colleges due to an exceptionally high demand from the ever increasing population) creates problems of poor health standards and poor education standards.
- *Literacy rates* (the percentage of the population which can read and write) are usually quite low.

Consequences of **falling birth rates** in developed countries include:

- *Under-population*. Where the birth rates and death rates are very low and are almost the same, population growth is very slow and is, in some cases, decreasing. When this happens the population structure becomes imbalanced.
- With fewer young people and an ever increasing number of older people there is greater pressure on the economically active age groups to support the dependent groups.
- Reasons for this structure include:
  - widespread use of artificial birth control
  - changes in the status of women, with many women having jobs and careers in preference to marrying young and starting a family
  - the change in attitudes of younger people towards marriage and size of families and the opportunities for improving the standard of living through having fewer children.

Migration Patterns

Key Point 8

You should be able to explain 'push and pull' factors of migration, both within a single country and between two countries, and discuss factors which can create barriers to migration

The factors that encourage people to leave the rural areas are termed **'rural push'** factors and those which attract people to the towns and cities are termed **'urban pull'** factors.

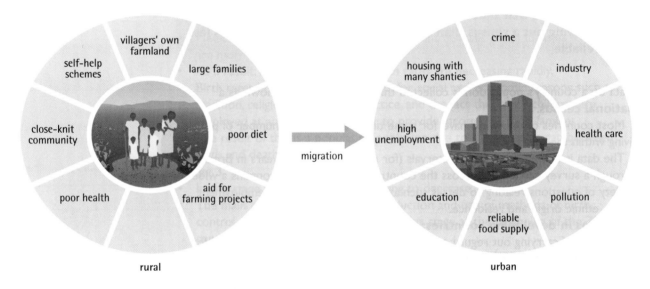

Figure 5·4 – Rural push and urban pull factors / associated problems in urban areas

Rural push factors include:
- Lack of good farming conditions such as poor soils, dry climate, difficult terrain.
- Loss of farmland through, for example, land reform measures or inability to repay debts.
- Lack of employment through increased use of mechanisation.
- Low wages from agricultural employment and therefore low standard of living. Poor living conditions. Possible lack of educational opportunities. Lack of facilities such as cinemas / theatres and other attractions, especially for younger generations.
- Quality of healthcare may be severely limited through lack of hospitals and medical staff. In some cases, problems with natural disasters such as floods, famine and droughts.

Urban pull factors include:
- Possibility of employment in a variety of jobs including manufacturing and service industries.
- Possibility of higher wages and therefore a higher standard of living. Offer of better housing conditions.
- Possibility of better educational opportunities for younger people. Wider range of attractions such as shops, entertainment and other services.
- Possibility of family and friends already living in urban areas offering encouragement.
- Possibility of better healthcare through more hospitals, clinics, doctors etc.

Migration barriers:
- Barriers to migration include legislation in receiving countries which limit the number of immigrants permitted to enter the country.
- Legislation may include references to marital status, ability to speak language of receiving country, professional or trade qualifications, political considerations or criminal records. Social barriers may include racial bias, problems with housing, education, employment and ethnic integration.

> ### Key Point 9
> **You should be able to discuss the advantages and disadvantages that migration has brought to both the losing and receiving countries**

Advantages:
- Receiving countries acquire labour for a variety of occupations, many of which may be less popular and difficult to fill from their own populations, or for which they have a skills shortage. The home countries of the immigrants benefit from money sent back and from skills that have been acquired when they return. There is also reduced pressure on resources while they are away.
- Incoming immigrants may add to the depth of culture of the existing population in terms of customs, language and traditions.
- If the receiving country's population is in decline, the immigrant population may help to reverse the trend, providing more balance to the population structure.

Disadvantages:
- Emigration creates problems for people living in the areas that lose people.
- In small communities such as rural villages (e.g. in the highlands of Scotland and villages in southern Italy and rural India), the loss of young people results in a highly imbalanced population structure.
- There is a large number of old people left. Often within a few years the community may eventually die out and the settlement may disappear.
- Immigration into new areas, whether it is a country or a city, often results in serious problems due to the pressures created on the existing population.
- New immigrants may increase the demand for housing, employment, education, healthcare and will obviously compete with the existing population for these services. In areas of relatively high unemployment, additional competition for employment (especially if the new immigrants are willing to work for less money) creates great resentment.

- Demand for accommodation causes problems, especially if the government is unable to supply the immigrants with housing.
- In developing countries the main result of this has been the emergence of shanty towns.
- In developed countries, immigration from other countries can result in racial problems between ethnic communities, especially where language differences exist.
- Racial discrimination is often common and shows itself in prejudice in employment, housing and in open racial abuse.

GEOGRAPHICAL METHODS AND TECHNIQUES

Key Point 10

You should be familiar with a variety of population graphs and be able to interpret them

Analysing different types of graphs is important in the study of population. For example, the analysis of the population model by reference to the different patterns of birth rates and death rates throughout the four different stages could be used to assess your geographical skills in this topic area.

This would involve being able to take each stage in turn and provide an analysis of whether the rates are rising or falling, how fast or slowly this is happening and what the net effect would be on population growth. Note that you could be expected to explain why these changes are occurring as well as describing what is happening.

In the external examination this question could be combined with a question requiring you to explain the patterns in the different stages and / or comment on the effects of these changes on the population as in the question you have looked at above.

You would draw on your knowledge of population trends, patterns and the factors responsible to help you explain population changes and their effects. You should be able to relate these to countries you have studied.

Interpretation of population data

- This skill involves being able to use population data to explain trends. Questions on these kinds of diagrams may ask you to examine the graphs, tables or maps and draw conclusions. For example, you may be given a table showing various measurements of population for two or more countries. This data may contain details on life expectancy, birth and death rates, infant mortality rates and other indicators such as medical provision.

- You may be asked to explain differences between the countries, e.g. differences in life expectancy.

- You can do this by firstly describing the differences and then referring to other information to support your conclusions on varying levels of development between the countries.

- Similarly if you are asked to use diagrams such as population pyramids to explain differences between countries, you should be able to identify patterns of birth and death rates and life expectancy rates and to match them appropriately to countries which are either developed (EMDCs) or developing (ELDCs).

- Your knowledge of factors which contribute to levels of development should help you to explain both the structures and the reasons for them.

SAMPLE QUESTIONS, ANSWERS, COMMENTS AND MARKING INSTRUCTIONS

Question 1

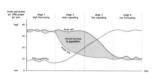

Reference Diagram Q1

(Stages of the Demographic Transition Model)

Study Reference Diagram Q1 (See Figure 5·3 on page 95), which shows the four stages in the Demographic Transition Model.
Referring to a country or countries which you have studied, describe and account for the changes in population from the beginning of stage 2 to the end of stage 3.
8 marks

Sample answer – 1

✓ denotes correct point

> There are four stages to the Demographic Transition Model but the two stages I am interested in are the early expanding and late expanding stage which are stages 2 and 3.
> In many countries in Africa like Ethiopia, Mali, Somalia etc. they're going through these stages at this moment in time.
> Stage 2 is the early expanding stage where after a high birth and death rate in stage one ✓ the death rate drops dramatically ✓. This is due to the introduction of many things. One of which is healthcare ✓, as before many people were dying of diseases which could be cured with simple vaccinations ✓ like whooping cough ✓ so less people die from the disease. The water sanitation has also been improved ✓ as people begin to separate waste from clean water and by doing this diseases are reduced ✓ as people now have clean water available. People's standard of life has improved ✓ but the birth rate remains high ✓ as people still produce babies as they did earlier so their family live on and at this stage the population dramatically increases ✓ due to a lot more people dying than being born.
> In stage 3 the death rate is low ✓ and the birth rate drops ✓ as people in countries like Ethiopia now realise that life is better and less babies die at a young rate so they begin to produce less babies as this would mean that they would not be able to afford food if the babies were still being born.
> The introduction of family planning and providing the families with condoms and other contraceptive methods ✓ come into play. The population at this point is still increasing ✓ but beginning to level off as birth rate reduces to alongside death rate.

Comments and marks obtained – 1

This is basically a good, sound answer covering the essential points in both parts of the question. However the answer is spoiled by several unnecessary additional statements such as the introductory sentence. There is also a certain amount of carelessness in parts of the answer in, for example, part two when referring to Ethiopia as an example for a stage 3 country. The last sentence in part one referring to 'more people dying than being born' is again confused and careless. Throughout the answer there are many relevant points such as good examples of stage 2 countries, death rate dropping dramatically, reference to healthcare and people dying from simple diseases. The comments on water sanitation reducing disease and the fact that there is an increase in population is credited.

In the comments on stage 3, the candidate correctly refers to low death rate and a falling birth rate and the link between quality of life and number of babies born. Comments on family planning and contraception are also worth additional marks as are the final statements on the growth rate levelling off due to parity between birth and death rates.

There are sufficient points made to gain a total of $15 \times \frac{1}{2}$ marks giving $7\frac{1}{2}$ out of **8** marks.

Question 2

Study reference Map Q2.

With reference to an example of a population migration between two named countries which you have studied:

(*a*) explain the migration in terms of 'push' and 'pull' factors and

(*b*) discuss the advantages and disadvantages which the migration has brought to either

(*i*) the 'losing' country or

(*ii*) the 'receiving' country

9 marks

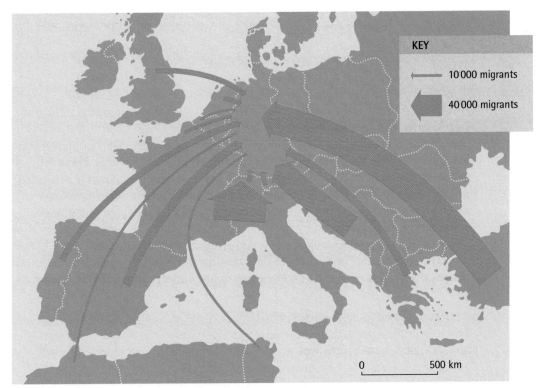

Reference Map Q2 – Migration to former West Germany in the mid 1970s

Sample answer – 2(a)

> Migration of the Turks into West Germany was brought on by a variety of factors. In Turkey there was a high unemployment rate ✓ and poor living conditions ✓. Germany offered plenty of work ✓, higher wages ✓, and better conditions. Although everything started off well, when Germany was reunited, the East Germans were looking for work and were angry at the Turks for taking the available jobs. This led to fighting and abuse toward the Turks by some antisocial groups.
>
> The German government had introduced restrictions on immigrants ✓ entering the country and have offered grants to Turks ✓ willing to leave the country.

Comments and marks obtained – 2(a)

This is a good example of an answer which contains many good points which unfortunately do not gain any credit since they do not answer the question being asked. The first references to high unemployment, poor living conditions and offers of work with higher wages merit marks.

The next section on East Germans etc., is irrelevant to the question asked and therefore receives no further marks despite making some good points.

Restrictions on immigrants is relevant and receives further credit.

In total the answer is worth $6 \times \frac{1}{2}$ marks giving a total of 3 out of 5 marks.

Sample answer – 2(b)

> The advantages for Germany were that the Turks were willing to do the unskilled ✓, dirty jobs that nobody else wanted ✓ at the time for a low wage ✓. It has been said that without the Turks, Germany's hospitals, electricity and transport services would cease ✓ to work.
>
> Disadvantages are the fighting and social problems where the Turks don't mingle with the Germans ✓ and introduced their own culture into the city.

Comments and marks obtained – 2(b)

The answer is credited for the references to the type of jobs taken by immigrants and that no one in the host country was willing to do them. Further credit is gained for mention of the low wages and that certain service industries depended on this labour. A final mark is obtained by the mention of the social problems which arise although the last part about culture could be seen as an advantage rather than a disadvantage.

A total of $5 \times \frac{1}{2}$ marks would be awarded giving $2\frac{1}{2}$ marks out of 4.

The whole mark for both parts of the question amounts to a total of 5 marks out of a possible 9. The answer is therefore worth just slightly more than the basic pass.

Marking instructions

Question 1

Answers to this question will be influenced by the candidate's choice of country or countries.

The answer should be assessed out of 8 allowing up to a maximum of 4 marks for description.

Stage 2

Countries could include UK up to the late 19ᵗʰ century or poorer countries in the developing world such as Bangladesh or Ethiopia.

There is a high birth rate due to factors such as –

- lack of birth control / family planning;
- parents wanting many children as an insurance policy due to high infant mortality rates;
- children can look after parents in their old age;
- more children means more income from working in industry or agriculture or helping on the farm;
- lack of education about modern family planning methods
- impact of religious beliefs encouraging larger families.

Death rates may show a marked decline due to –

- improvements in medical care (new drugs, vaccinations, clinics etc.);
- improved sanitation and water supply;
- increased food production and more balanced diets;
- decrease in infant mortality rates; more people living into middle age / life expectancy increasing.

The rate of population increase leads to a 'population explosion'

Stage 3

Countries could include UK in late 19ᵗʰ century up to about World War 2 or developing countries such as India, China or Egypt.

The population structure is more evenly balanced with increased life expectancy due to –

- declining death rates due to improvements outlined above (stage 2);
- gradual slowing down of birth rates leading to a gradual slowing down of population growth rate.

The fall in birth rates may be due to –

- changing attitudes towards children as 'economic liabilities rather than assets'.
- an increasing awareness and availability of family planning measures in many developing countries; government policies designed to limit births (e.g. one child policy in China).

Question 2
Assess out of 9 allowing up to 5 marks for either part (*a*) or part (*b*).
Answers must refer to both 'push and pull' factors for full marks.
If no specific is migration mentioned, assess out of 4.
Answers to both parts will obviously depend on the migration selected.

2(*a*) Push factors might include –
- lack of job opportunities / prospects in own country;
- political or religious persecution;
- poor standard of living in own country.

Pull factors might include –
- prospects of earning higher wages;
- better employment opportunity;
- perceived better quality of life;
- family or friends already in new country.

2(*b*) Answers again depend on migration chosen but must refer to both advantages and disadvantages for full marks.

Either **2(*b*) (*i*)** Advantages to donor country, e.g Turkey might include –
- additional income being sent home;
- reduces pressure on jobs and resources;
- possible decline in birth rate with loss of people of child bearing age;
- eventual return of migrants with new skills and supply of capital.

Disadvantages to donor country, e.g. Turkey –
- loss of people most likely to have education and skills;
- mostly males who leave leading to family problems;
- population imbalance;
- more elderly population left behind with less income to support them.

Or **2(*b*) (*ii*)** Advantages to receiving country, e.g. (West) Germany might include –
- immigrant labourers helped overcome labour shortage in post WW2;
- Turks were willing to undertake more menial jobs for lower rewards;
- helped build the economy after ravages of war.

Disadvantages might include –
- problems of integration;
- racial unrest leading to violence;
- additional pressure on social services, education etc.
- problems increased after reunification of Germany with increased demands for jobs from former East German people.

GLOSSARY OF ASSOCIATED TERMS

Active population: That section of the population of a country which is economically active/working.

Birth rate: The number of live births per thousand of the population in any country in any year.

Census: A numerical count of the population financed and carried out by the government at set periods of time, e.g. 10 year intervals.

Death rate: The number of deaths per thousand of the population of any country in any given year.

Population density: The average number of people within a given area, e.g. 100 per square kilometre.

Developed country: Sometimes referred to as 'economically more developed countries (EMDCs)' include countries which have a high standard of living or high physical quality of life.

Developing countries: Often referred to as 'economically less developed countries (ELDCs)' in which the population generally has a low standard of living.

Empty lands: Areas of the world which have a low population density, e.g. mountains and deserts.

Environmental factors: Factors such as climate, relief, soil and water supply which can influence the distribution of population in an area.

Gross Domestic Product (GDP): The value of all goods and services of a country produced in one year and is used as an indicator of the wealth of a country. However it does not always reveal how well spread the wealth is among the population in general.

Infant mortality: The number of children below the age of one year which die per thousand of the population.

Life expectancy: The average age a person can expect to live in any given country. This is a good indicator of level of development, since people in more developed countries tend to live longer due to better healthcare, better diets, higher standards of education and housing etc.

Population structure: This refers to the grouping of the population of a country by age and sex. Inspection of the structure may also indicate trends in birth and death rates, life expectancy and the possible impact of factors such as war and migration on the population.

Population growth model: This shows different stages of population growth based on the relationship between birth and death rates.

Standard of living: This is the level of economic well-being of people in a country.

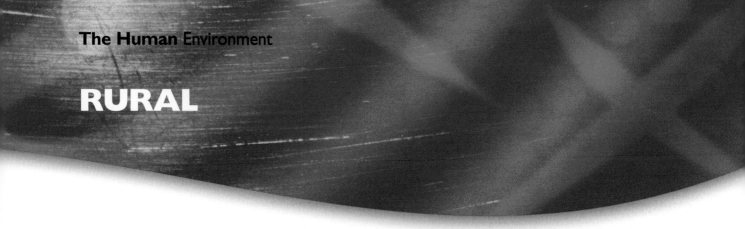

RURAL

The main aspects of this topic area which you need to learn involve knowledge of agricultural systems in different parts of the world and the types of landscapes associated with these systems. You should also know how these systems and landscapes can change, the reasons for the changes and the implications of any changes.

AGRICULTURAL SYSTEMS

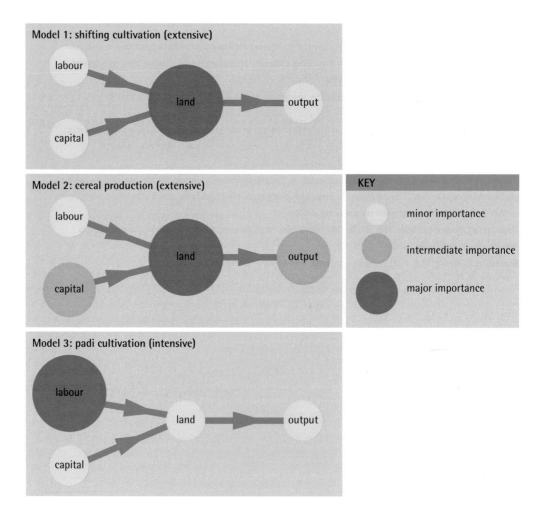

Figure 6·1 – Models of selected agricultural systems

Any system involves **inputs**, **processes** and **outputs**.

In farming, inputs include physical factors such as climate, landscape and soils; human factors such as population, land ownership and cultural background; and economic factors such as capital investment, technology, government influence, transport and markets.

Outputs include the crops, livestock and all other farm produce.

Certain processes occur between the input and output stages. These processes involve a range of activities which depend on the type of farm and the end product.

The type of farm which operates depends on decisions taken by the farmer which are influenced by various inputs.

For example in the UK, in an area where soil quality is relatively poor, climate is difficult and the landscape is rugged, the decision might be taken to opt for rearing sheep as opposed to any other type of farming.

For the purposes of the examination, you need to know about three particular farming systems: shifting cultivation, intensive peasant farming and extensive commercial farming.

Figure 6·1 shows models of these systems.

> ### Key Point 1
> **You should be able to describe the main features of the system of Shifting cultivation and explain the population density associated with the system**

Agricultural System 1 – shifting cultivation

Shifting cultivation is the name given to the system of farming found mainly in the tropical rainforests and is one of the most primitive types of agriculture practised today.

Basically, the system involves a group of people clearing an area in the rainforest and growing various crops until the soil becomes exhausted. When this happens, the group leave the area and move to another part of the forest and begin the process over again. The area which is left starts to regenerate after a period of about seven years.

Inputs
Inputs consist of areas of cleared forest land and manual labour.

Processes
* The natural forest is cleared either by cutting down the trees or by burning them.
* A fairly large area is cleared to allow some parts to be cultivated, whilst other areas are left fallow to maintain fertility.
* Ash from the burned trees provides some fertiliser for the soils.
* The crops are planted in the ash-covered ground.
* As the soil becomes less fertile due to continuous growing of crops, other crops which can grow in less fertile soils are grown.
* Other processes involve clearing, burning, planting and harvesting. As one part of the clearing becomes infertile it is abandoned and a new area is farmed.

Outputs
- Outputs may include crops such as yams and manioc, fruit trees, coca beans and sometimes tobacco.
- As the yield decreases over the years and the ground becomes more and more infertile, the whole site is abandoned. The group or tribe then moves to another area and the process begins over again.
- The whole system is geared to supply the food requirements of the tribe and is not at all commercial.
- Diet can be supplemented by food obtained either by hunting, fishing or gathering fruits and plants within the surrounding area.
- Although primitive in terms of methods and technology the whole process actually is very well suited to areas with difficult environmental conditions such as poor soils.
- The added advantage is that shifting cultivation can be environmentally friendly in that, given time, the forest can recover.
- Deforestation is only temporary. However, if some parts of the clearing are over-farmed, the soil can become exhausted and leached and may not recover.

Key Point 2

You should be able to describe the main landscape features of this system

Landscape of shifting cultivation:
- Temporary shelter is provided by huts and only parts of the area are actually under cultivation at any given time, with large areas left as fallow.
- The whole area may use as much as 20 acres. Several clearings may be made as the soil loses its fertility. A total area of up to 100 acres may be needed to support a group of about 20 to 25 people.
- Different parts are farmed at different times over a period of several years, perhaps up to 10 years.
- Since the land can support only a limited number of people, population density is low with this system of farming.
- Tribes are usually quite small and widely scattered throughout the forest leading to quite a low population density.

Key Point 3

You should be able to describe changes to the system, discuss benefits and problems resulting from the changes and assess the impact of changes on people and their ways of life and the landscape

Rural change affecting shifting cultivation:
- Shifting cultivators have had to compete with other land uses within the forests.
- Mining, ranching, settlement, roads, plantations and hydro-electric schemes have all increased the pressure on these primitive farmers.
- The shifting cultivators have been forced to move further and deeper into the forest. As the amount of land decreases the time which land is allowed to remain fallow is more limited. Consequently the clearings have to be abandoned earlier as the soil is unable to maintain sufficient fertility to grow the necessary crops. In some cases the tribes are forced to abandon the system altogether and seek an alternative form of existence.
- In some areas, for example in parts of the Amazon, the tribes have been forced to move into reservations. Their traditional way of life is therefore threatened by coming into contact with modern civilisation. The natives have been badly affected by their lack of immunity to western diseases and this is reflected in the falling populations. Even simple diseases, such as common colds and measles, can have devastating effects.
- Gradually many shifting cultivators are being absorbed into the advancing 'civilised' culture and have become sedentary farmers, albeit reluctantly.
- Some of the tribes seek work on the plantations, others in forestry. In many areas this system is gradually being destroyed although some governments, (e.g. Brazil) have tried to restore the rights and traditions of shifting cultivators.
- However these efforts may be too little and too late and the power of large scale commercial development too great to resist.
- Despite these changes it is estimated that up to 200 million people still remain in the system of shifting cultivation throughout the world.
- Clearly there is considerable resistance to change and a tremendous desire to retain this way of life.

Agricultural system 2 – Intensive Peasant Farming

Key Point 4
You should be able to describe the main features of the system of Intensive peasant farming and explain the associated population density

This type of farming is found throughout south east Asia including India. Several different types of crops may be grown depending on climatic conditions. In wetter areas, rice is the main crop. There are several different varieties of rice which can be grown but the most important is wet rice.

Since the growing season is comparatively short (100 days at temperatures above 20°C), in areas where the rainfall is available throughout the year or where crops can be irrigated, two or three crops can be grown in a single year.

Inputs

- Inputs include physical factors such as flat land or, where this is limited, terraces on slopes; impervious soils; and sufficient water to flood the fields in which the rice is grown.
- These are known as rice padi fields.
- Natural fertiliser may be added after the seeds are planted.

Processes

- If the fields are flooded, the floods may deposit silt which adds to the fertility of the soil.
- Where rainfall is deficient, irrigation in various forms is used to bring additional water to the fields. Irrigation methods are fairly primitive, involving for example inundation canals led from nearby rivers or from makeshift dams.
- Seeds grown earlier in nursery beds are transplanted to the fields which are under several centimetres of water.
- Stone walls are built around fields to retain water.
- The system is highly labour-intensive throughout all stages including seeding, fertilising and harvesting. Most of the work is done by hand.
- To help maintain fertility of the soil, rice stubble is ploughed back into the fields. Other fertiliser is added including algae which floats on the water and animal manure if it is available.
- Soil erosion is prevented by the building of embankments to protect the fields or terraces to prevent soil creep.
- There is very little use of machinery in any of these stages. Livestock such as cattle are used as draught animals to pull ploughs and carts.
- The fields are allowed to dry out when the crop matures to allow the rice to ripen.
- Due to the fact that the system is highly labour intensive, population density is usually very high in areas with this system of farming.
- The land tenure system whereby farmers have inherited small plots of land from their fathers makes it difficult to use mechanisation due to the size of fields.
- Although the system may provide just enough food for those who farm the land, the process is largely inefficient and output is highly variable.
- Large families mean children can be used as extra labour at no extra cost.

Output

- Rice is the main crop grown in the wetter areas.
- The most important variety is the 'wet' rice grown in flooded fields.
- Usually two crops are grown each year on the best land.
- Other crops include wheat and maize.
- In drier areas, for example the interior of the Indian sub-continent, crops grown under drier conditions include cereal crops such as wheat, millet and sorghum, chick peas and in some areas, manioc.
- Manure is provided by cattle for fertiliser.

Key Point 5
You should be able to describe the main features of the landscape of peasant farming

Figure 6·2 – Typical peasant farming landscape

The main features which you should be able to describe include:
- Fields which are usually very small due to the land tenure system.
- Rice being planted under water.
- There is a distinct lack of mechanisation and therefore a high number of workers working in the fields planting and harvesting crops by hand.
- The use of irrigation ditches to transfer water to fields, especially in drier areas.
- The use of animals such as oxen to draw carts and transport crops.
- Embankments are built to retain water in the fields.
- Slopes are terraced to maximise the use of land and to conserve soil and water content.

Key Point 6

You should be able to describe changes in crop production and suggest why this has occurred, referring to, for example, the Green Revolution

There have been various attempts by governments of countries with peasant farming to introduce modern methods and changes to areas which practise this system of farming, for example, the Punjab.

These measures have been described as the **Green Revolution**. The main features of the Green Revolution are summarised in Figure 6·3.

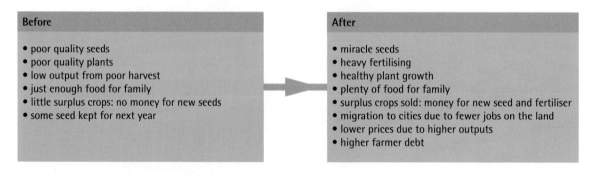

Before	After
• poor quality seeds • poor quality plants • low output from poor harvest • just enough food for family • little surplus crops: no money for new seeds • some seed kept for next year	• miracle seeds • heavy fertilising • healthy plant growth • plenty of food for family • surplus crops sold: money for new seed and fertiliser • migration to cities due to fewer jobs on the land • lower prices due to higher outputs • higher farmer debt

Figure 6·3 – Green Revolution main features

The Indian government introduced various schemes to improve farming during programmes of 5 and 7 year plans.

This involved a range of measures including:

*   Land reform schemes whereby small farms resulting from the land inheritance system have been amalgamated into larger farms.
*   Schemes to encourage farmers to borrow money to improve their farms.
*   Introduction of miracle seeds in order to increase yields.
*   Using chemical fertilisers to improve soil fertility.
*   Increasing mechanisation by using tractors and other farm machinery.
*   Employing agricultural advisers and setting up various training schemes for farmers.
*   Spraying insecticides on to crops to prevent crops being eaten and destroyed by insects.
*   Introducing modern irrigation methods to replace inefficient methods such as inundation canals.
*   Raising the level of technology used on farms such as introducing motorised ploughs.
*   Introducing legislation designed to increase the size of fields and allow the system to use large machinery and become more efficient.

Key Point 7
You should be able to discuss the implications of these changes on people and the landscape and comment on their success or otherwise

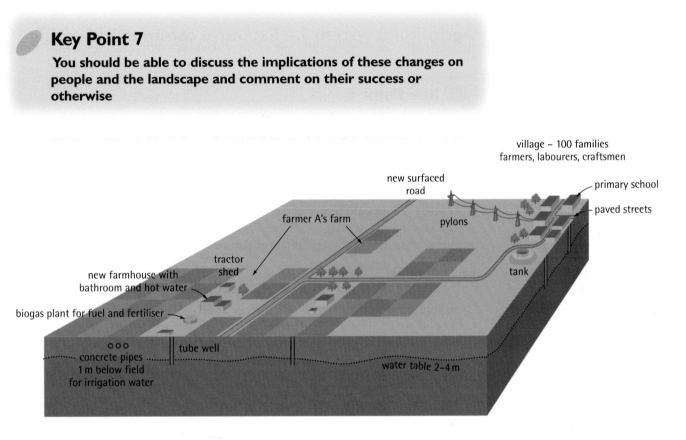

Figure 6·4 – Modern agricultural landscape in South Asia

- All of these measures were designed to increase yield and output from the farms. The changes brought about by the Green Revolution have had some success, for example in India during the 1970s and 1980s. As a result of the uptake of Green Revolution techniques, production doubled during these decades.
- The changes also brought problems. Use of fertilisers, pesticides and other new techniques cost farmers a great deal of money. Farmers were encouraged to borrow money from banks to supplement government loans and grants.
- As yields increased prices fell due to increased supply. Many farmers did not earn enough money to both achieve a reasonable income and be able to repay the money they had borrowed.
- Only the richer farmers benefited. Mechanisation left many farmers unemployed.
- Consequently many farmers had to give up their farms, leaving to migrate to other areas or large cities.
- Land reform, although helping to speed up the process of mechanisation and modernisation, basically deprived many farmers of the opportunity to own their own farms and thus have at least a chance of providing food for their families.
- The Green Revolution has been successful in some areas where land reform was successful. In other areas the success rate has been much lower and in some cases many farmers have become poorer as a direct result of the Green Revolution.

Agricultural system 3 – Extensive commercial farming

> **Key Point 8**
>
> **You should be able to describe the system of Extensive Commercial Farming, describe its landscape and explain recent changes to the system and their effects**

The main purpose of this kind of system of farming is to produce output from the farm which is sold both in the domestic and the export market, making large profits. This type of farming is generally found in the temperate regions of North America, South America, Western Europe, Australia and South Africa.

Physical inputs
- *Landscape* – As noted earlier, the land is generally flat. This aids mechanisation in the ploughing and harvesting of the crops and in transporting the produce.
- *Soils* – The soil quality in most commercial farming areas is generally very good. Soils are often rich in humus, deep and very fertile such as the black earth soils of the prairies and the Steppes of the Ukraine.
- *Climate* – Summers are usually warm; precipitation levels are high enough without being too high and precipitation occurs mainly during the growing season. Soils are broken up by frosts in winter. Occasionally some areas such as the prairies suffer climatic hazards such as drought, early frosts and tornadoes.

Human inputs
The main input into this system is capital. Capital input includes:
- *Land* – An extensive acreage of land that can be in excess of several thousand square kilometres in the case of ranching in U.S.A and Australia, and between one and two hundred hectares in the prairies of N. America. The land on the grain farms is usually very flat.
- *Mechanisation* – Extensive grain farms make use of modern machinery including combine harvesters, ploughs and aircraft to spray crops with insecticides.
- *Fertilisers / pesticides* – Although crops and cattle are cultivated in many areas where the soil is rich and fertile, nevertheless vast sums of money are spent on artificial fertilisers and pesticides.
- *Transport* – Extensive grain farming greatly depends on the availability of a highly efficient transport (rail / water) network for the distribution of the produce to markets both home and abroad.
- *Improved seeds* – Seeds that can produce higher yields and can be resistant to climatic factors such as drought and frost are used extensively.
- *Selective irrigation* – Although the climatic conditions in terms of rainfall are normally more than sufficient for the needs of the farms, there are some areas that require to supplement the rainfall with irrigation schemes.
- *Labour* – Unlike other types of farming, the labour input into extensive commercial farming is low due to the system being highly mechanised. Output per person is relatively high. Population density in areas with this type of agriculture is quite low and, as mechanisation increases, population continues to decline.

- *Political* – Governments greatly influence the operation of commercial farms. This is achieved through several measures including providing grants; subsidies; making trading alliances with other countries such as the EU; agreeing tariffs to protect farmers; providing colleges and agricultural training and research centres; and making economic decisions that can affect local, national and international prices.

Processes / Methods

Processes involved in commercial farming include:

- Ploughing, fertilising, planting, harvesting, storage, transportation, maintenance of machinery.
- Strip farming (ploughing land at right angles to the wind) with wheat and grass grown in alternate strips is becoming more common.
- Farmers often hire squads of specialist workers with combine harvesters rather than harvest their own crops. All stages of production are carefully monitored to make the system as financially efficicient as possible.
- Crop farms invest heavily in a variety of buildings for livestock and storage purposes. A great deal of money is also invested in the protection of livestock and produce from disease, e.g. insecticides and veterinary costs.
- Other processing costs involve the construction of processing plants; advertising and marketing; and continual research into improving farming methods and techniques.
- Produce is transported mainly by rail to ports and other cities.

Outputs

- In the Canadian prairies output consists mainly of spring wheat and cattle, although other crops include barley and sugar beet.
- Winter wheat, planted in winter and harvested in autumn, is grown in warmer areas furhter south.
- Fodder crops such as alfalfa are also grown for large cattle ranches.

Landscape

- Figure 6·5 shows the field patterns and landscape typical of a large scale commercial farming area and is based on a wheat farming area in the American Plain lands.
- Farms growing cereal crops tend to have large, very regular field patterns.

Figure 6·5 – Typical field pattern – commercial grain farming

- Farms have been amalgamated in large units often in excess of 400 hectares.
- In the Midwestern states of the U.S.A. such as Wisconsin and Iowa, the fields are laid out in large rectangular blocks measuring sometimes over a hundred acres (40 hectares) each. This figure can rise to over 300 hectares in some areas.

Key Point 9

You should be able to describe changes to Extensive Commercial Agriculture and comment on the benefits and problems caused by these changes

- Capital input in this type of farming has always been high in terms of land and machinery.
- This has continually increased especially in terms of mechanisation.
- More recently, instead of farmers buying their own machines such as combine harvesters, the trend has been to either operate within a cooperative or alternatively hire companies that supply labour and machines such as combine harvesters at harvest time.
- Hiring machinery and labour is more cost-effective for farmers than than buying their own machines and carrying out the harvesting jobs themselves.
- These companies that provide labour and machines migrate northwards during the summer months according to the time of year when the cereals ripen. The increase in mechanisation has resulted in further reductions in labour input. This, in turn, has led to a reduction in population within areas with this type of farming.
- Different types of seeds that have improved disease-resistant and faster-growing properties have also been introduced. This has resulted in higher crop yields each year.
- Yields have also been increased through the use of increased amounts of fertilisers and pesticides. The relatively recent innovation of genetically-modified crops has also been a further change in the farming process although this step is highly controversial.
- Infrastructure has to be continually improved so as to speed up the process of transporting crops to markets.
- Measures to improve road and railway services are constantly being reviewed with a view to increasing efficiency. For example, wheat is stored in huge elevators which are linked to the railway transport system.
- Diversification is another change being introduced into the system. Various other crops and produce have been added to the output of extensive commercial farms such as sugar beet, beef and dairy produce.
- Problems that result from this approach include the fact that smaller farmers find it increasingly difficult to compete with larger enterprises in terms of increasing capital input and matching the efficiency of the bigger units.
- Smaller farmers have therefore had to sell their farmers to their larger competitors.
- Those formerly employed in farming have lost their jobs due to increased mechanisation and have had to find alternative employment or leave the area altogether in search of work.
- Population density has therefore decreased in some areas.

Key Point 10

You should be able to describe and explain the settlement patterns which have resulted from this type of farming

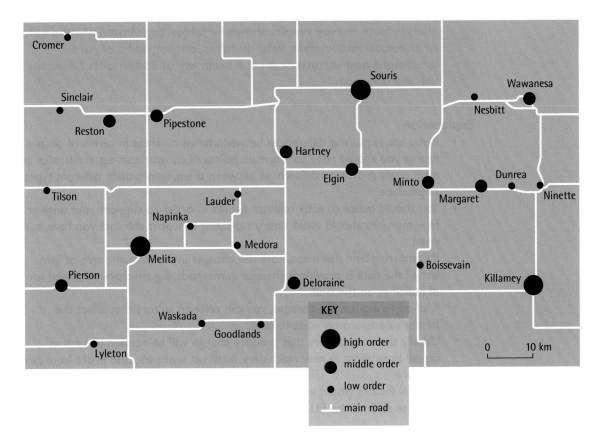

Figure 6·6 – Settlement patterns

Settlement has evolved in a recognisable pattern of a regular spacing arrangement. There can be seen to be a hierarchy of settlements, ranging from hamlets to towns, with fewer larger settlements providing services for the larger number of smaller settlements.

This spacing is partly due to the field patterns, the road and railway networks and the service function of the settlements.

Farmers export their grain through the railway network, therefore the towns are distributed along the railway lines in a linear fashion. The flat landscape allows people to have equal access in all directions along the road system.

Regular spacing of the service centres ensures that each centre maximises their share of the available consumers in the area who use the towns to purchase goods and services.

Flat land; commercial farming; and towns that act as service centres in a hierarchical order are the main factors that produce this settlement pattern.

SAMPLE QUESTIONS, ANSWERS, COMMENTS AND MARKING INSTRUCTIONS

Question 1

'Despite its declining importance, it is estimated that approximately 200 million people are still dependent on some form of shifting agriculture'.

With reference to an area you have studied,

(a) describe the main characteristics of shifting agriculture and,
5 marks

(b) explain why this system of farming is changing and assess the impact of the changes on the lifestyles of the people.
5 marks
(10 marks)

Sample answer – 1(a)
✓ denotes correct point

> Shifting cultivation is mainly found in the Rainforests ✓ – small clearings are made by chopping down a few trees ✓ (not fruit trees).
> Some trees are kept to provide shelter ✓ from the tropical storms and to prevent a loss of soil and fertility.
> Small nucleated villages are situated around the clearing ✓.
> All materials the Indians use come from the forest, no waste.
> Little machines are used ✓, everything is done by hand.
> After crop production, clearing is abandoned ✓ in order for soil to regenerate.
> The method is labour intensive ✓, very sparsely populated ✓.

Comments and marks obtained – 1(a)
In answers such as these, it is difficult to separate explanations of low population density from descriptions of the type of farming practised. Therefore, although this answer only refers to population density near the end, the description of the characteristics of the farming system closely links the explanation of population density to the features of the system. Therefore credit is given for references to location in the Rainforest (difficult environment), small clearings made by felling trees, trees kept for shelter, small nucleated villages, little use of machines, abandonment of clearing after cropping, labour intensive methods and sparse population. The candidate could have added that the size of the clearing and the methods used could only support a small population and this would have most definitely have linked description and explanation.
In total the answer obtained $8 \times \frac{1}{2}$ marks giving 4 marks out of 5.

Sample answer – 1(b)

This system of farming is changing as people are coming from other countries to use the land, for tree chopping ✓ and mining ✓, The Indians have less land to farm, so less clearings can be produced resulting in overworked, over used soils ✓.

These changes have a huge impact on the lifestyles of the inhabitants of the rainforest.

Indians are forced to move to larger cities ✓ as more machines are used and there is no need for many jobs ✓.

The White man has brought disease like the common cold or measles and alcoholism ✓ to the Indians who have no immunisation to these trivial diseases and die from them ✓.

Traditional methods of cultivation are replaced by mechanical methods ✓ and the old ways are forgotten by the future children ✓.

The changes in the farming has serious consequences for the Indians and their lifestyle.

Comments and marks obtained – 1(b)

The answer has sufficient detail to merit a good pass. Marks are obtained for the statements on other competing land uses – tree chopping and mining and a third mark for reference to over-used soils.

At this point the candidate could have elaborated on the increased effects of deforestation and the difficulties faced by shifting cultivators. Reference could have been made to the Indians having to abandon their way of life to seek employment in some of the other industries such as the rubber tapping, ranching and timber industries. Mention could also have been made of the shifting cultivators' gradual introduction of some modern technology albeit on a small scale, e.g. radios. This indicates the gradual 'civilisation' of the tribes.

The answer improves when discussing the impact and marks are gained for points relating to the movement of Indians to towns, the impact of diseases and their effects, the loss of traditional methods of farming and the effect on future generations.

Altogether the answer gained $9 \times \frac{1}{2}$ marks giving a total of $4\frac{1}{2}$ out of 5.

parts (a) and (b) together gave a total of $8\frac{1}{2}$ out of 10 for the question, well above the basic pass.

Question 2

(a) Describe three main features of either extensive commercial farming or intensive peasant farming.
3 marks

(b) Study Reference Table Q2A
The Green Revolution was an example of change in areas of intensive peasant farming.
For either the Punjab or another area of intensive peasant farming which you have studied,
　(i) describe the changes which have taken place, and
　(ii) comment on the successes and failures of these changes.
6 marks
(9 marks)

Reference Table Q2A (Agricultural change in the Punjab)

	1960	1970
Amount of land irrigated by tube wells (%)	35	70
Fertiliser Application (kg/hectare)	20	271
Area under high yielding varieties of wheat (hectares)	69	169,972
Wheat yields (kg/hectares)	1152	367

Sample answer – 2 (a)

> Intensive peasant farming has three main features as follows:
> It is usually carried out on small areas of land ✓ very intensively farmed ✓.
> There are many workers ✓ for each area of land and very little or no machinery is used ✓.
> It usually occurs in developing countries ✓ and often involves only one crop, e.g. rice ✓ in India.

Comments and marks obtained – 2 (a)

This answer contains sufficient detail to obtain $7\frac{1}{2}$ marks. These are gained for points relating to small areas, labour input per area, lack of machinery, location in developing countries and monoculture, i.e. one crop grown.
The answer obtains a total of $6 \times \frac{1}{2}$, i.e. 3 out of 3.

Sample answer – 2 (b) (i)

> In India the Green Revolution has had various degrees of success.
> Land which was previously 'fragmented' has been joined together ✓ and land less workers have been given sections of land ✓. The land owners land is no longer fragmented but is all in one area ✓.
> Machinery has been introduced ✓ and is used in areas, new irrigation methods ✓. Fertilisers and pesticides have been introduced ✓ and their uses have been shown to be succesful ✓.
> Farmers have been educated ✓ in the use of these new materials.
> new high yielding varieties (HYV) ✓ have been introduced to replace the old seeds.

Comments and marks obtained – 2 (b) (i)

The answer contains some comments which are not awarded any marks such as the first sentence. Marks are achieved for the statements on 'joining of previously fragmented land, workers given sections of land, machinery being introduced, new irrigation methods, fertilisers and pesticides, education of farmers and the introduction of new, high yielding varieties of seed'.

The answer has therefore been good enough to obtain a total of $7 \times \frac{1}{2}$ marks resulting in a total of $3\frac{1}{2}$ out of 3 marks. However only three marks are available for this part of the question, therefore the total marks gained is 3 out of 3.

Sample answer – 2 (b) (ii)

> The changes have been successful in some ways and unsuccessful in others. the new HYVs have been replaced by even higher yielding varieties ✓.
> The problem has been that only the already better off farmers have been able to afford the new HYVs ✓ and machinery and irrigation methods and have therefore increased their yields ✓ but the already poor farmers have been unable to afford ✓ these new things and therefore have become poorer because they cannot compete with the competitive prices ✓ the better off farmers provide. Or they have taken out loans ✓ with extortionate high interest rates ✓ and have been unable to repay them and ended up further in debt ✓.

Comments and marks obtained – 2 (b) (ii)

The answer contains more than sufficient points to earn pass marks. Points are gained for comments on 'higher yield varieties being introduced, only affordable by better off farmers as well as machinery / irrigation, increasing their yields, offered at competitive prices which poor farmers cannot compete with, resulting in loans which cannot be repaid causing further debt'.

This answer therefore obtains $8 \times \frac{1}{2}$ marks giving a total of 4 out of 6.

Overall the total marks for parts (a) and (b) amount to 8 out of a possible 9.

Marking instructions

Question 1

Assess out of 5, awarding a $\frac{1}{2}$ mark for each relevant statement.

1 (a) The main characteristics of shifting agriculture could include:
It involves temporary settlement of a cleared area – usually the more inaccessible and less exploited areas of rainforest – by a tribal / extended family group. Population densities are low; cultivation is of a subsistence nature and is supplemented by hunting and fishing; small areas of forest are cleared using primitive instruments; undergrowth is removed to prevent re-growth; felled trees are burned to provide ash for fertiliser – process is known as 'slash and burn'; staple crops include manioc grown in forest clearings called 'chagras'; several chagras may be in use at one time; other areas are left fallow to allow land to recover; high labour input is needed to provide sufficient food for a few people; therefore the system can only support a low population; within a few years soils become leached and yields decline and the sites are abandoned; the tribe shifts to another part of the forest and the process begins again; since the forest gradually recovers, the system is considered to be environmentally friendly.

1 (b) Assess out of 5 with up to 3 marks for either 'explanation of changes' or 'impact'.

Answers could refer to problems relating to development of rain forest, e.g. timber extraction, new roads, settlements, HEP schemes, ranching, mining.

Tribal lands are taken over resulting in loss of traditional way of life; tribes move deeper into the forest; they join homeless / landless / jobless people in shanty town outside urban areas; reduction in fallow areas leads to reduction in yield; some tribes people try to find employment in other activities; disease can affect people with no natural immunity to modern disease.

Question 2

2 (a) For full marks you should fully describe the three main features of your chosen system. Award a $\frac{1}{2}$ mark for each relevant point.

For example:

Intensive Peasant Farming:

This is usually a subsistence type of farming; the system requires a high input of labour; capital and land are much smaller by comparison with labour input; soil is usually quite fertile; climate often permits more than one crop per year; rice is often the main crop and has a relatively short growing season; the production for each unit area is often high; drier areas usually use some form of irrigation such as inundation canals; the high output can therefore support a high population.

Extensive Commercial Farming:

The system is geared to cash crops producing a good profit; input is mainly a large area of land with capital spent on machinery, fertiliser and pesticides; labour input is low due to use of mechanisation; output is fairly low overall; the system is dominated by the family unit; as a result population density is usually low due to mechanisation, output and climatic factors which only support individual farms.

2(b) (i) Possible changes might include:

Change to the land tenure system; this would allow small plots to be amalgamated to form larger areas; this would allow larger machines to be used, e.g. tractors; use of new irrigation schemes; introduction of high-yielding varieties of seeds; use of chemical fetilisers and pesticides.

2(b) (ii) Successes might include:

Greater yields each year; higher output meaning more food available for the population; incomes of farmers increasing with higher yields; more efficient use of machinery on larger fields; less damage to crops from insects; water for crops during dry seasons.

Failures may include: increasing debt for farmers as the borrow to pay for machinery, seeds, fertilisers, irrigation and pesticides; may result in farmers who cannot pay back loans losing their farms; as output increases, prices may fall, resulting in lower profits; poorer farmers may be unable to compete with richer land owners who may lower their prices to sell more.

GLOSSARY OF ASSOCIATED TERMS

Agribusiness: The operation of a large-scale farm, which resembles a factory, with large investments in farm property, maintenance, machinery and technology

Arable farming: Farms where the main activity and income source is the growing of crops.

Casual workers: Workers employed at specific times during the year (for example at harvesting times).

Cereal crops: Grain crops such as oats, barley or wheat.

Common Agricultural Policy (CAP): A system used by the European Union to give farmers guaranteed prices for their products.

Crofting: A type of mixed farming found in northern Scotland which is not very profitable; crofting farmers often have to supplement their income by taking on other part-time jobs.

Crop rotation: A system designed to maintain the fertility of soil by growing crops in different fields from time to time.

Dairying: Farming in which the produce is derived from milk. Cows are reared to supply milk on a daily basis. This system has become highly mechanised with milking machines, high standards of hygiene and milk lorries that take the milk to dairies where it is processed into various products. Farmers are paid on the amount of milk supplied.

Diversification: Adding different enterprises to the farm in order to improve income and allow the farmer to become less dependent on income from farm produce alone.

Drainage: If the underlying rock is clay, bogland and marshland may develop. Pipes are laid in order to drain excess water from the surface and allow the land to be farmed.

Farm system: The relationship between inputs, processes and outputs on a farm.

Fertilisers: Substances (organic or chemical-based) that are added to soil to increase its fertility and improve crop yields.

Fodder crops: Crops grown on a farm to feed animals (for example, grass and turnips).

Inputs: The basic needs of a farm before the farmer can begin to farm the land (such as seeds, livestock and machinery).

Insecticides: These may be sprayed on to crops to kill insects which may be attacking crops and therefore destroying the yield.

Mixed farms: Farms which are based on a combination of arable and pastoral farming including, for example, dairy farms.

Outputs: The end product from the inputs and the processes of production on the farm

Pastoral farm: Farms which are based on rearing livestock such as beef cattle farming and upland sheep farming.

Pasture: Land grazed by livestock. Some of this may be permanent, some temporary and some might be poor pasture which has been improved by, for example, underground drainage schemes.

Processes: This is all the work done on the farm. This obviously varies according to the type of farm.

Quotas: These are limits imposed on farmers in order to restrict the output of certain types of produce to avoid surpluses and therefore a drop in prices.

Rough grazing: Poor quality land used for grazing (for example upland areas where soil is thin and is grazed by sheep).

Root crops: Crops harvested for their roots such as potatoes, turnips and carrots.

INDUSTRY

Industry can be defined as the work which is done for economic gain. To help our understanding of this complex process, industry is usually classified into several different categories.

Key Point 1

You should know the different types of industry and be able to give examples of each type

Primary industry
These are the industries that extract raw materials directly from the earth. They include activities such as farming, forestry, quarrying and mining.

Secondary industry
These industries manufacture products from either raw materials or semi-finished products from other industries. These include iron and steel making, shipbuilding, petrochemicals, food-processing, engineering, electronics and motor vehicles.

Tertiary industry
These industries basically provide a service for consumers. They include retailing and wholesaling, transport and administration, financial and medical services, education and other trades and professions.

Quaternary industries
These include industries that are based on technological development including information technology, scientific research and development, and technological advice and expertise.

Key Point 2

You should be able to describe the main features of an industrial system

Inputs and outputs

All categories of industry operate as systems based on inputs, processes and outputs. These are summarised in the following flow diagram Figure 7·1

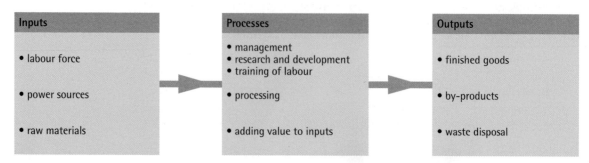

Inputs	Processes	Outputs
• labour force	• management • research and development • training of labour	• finished goods
• power sources	• processing	• by-products
• raw materials	• adding value to inputs	• waste disposal

Figure 7·1 – Industrial System

Key Point 3

You should know the factors which influence the location of different types of industry (primary, secondary, tertiary – old and new industry). You should also be able to explain the impact of each factor on specific industries

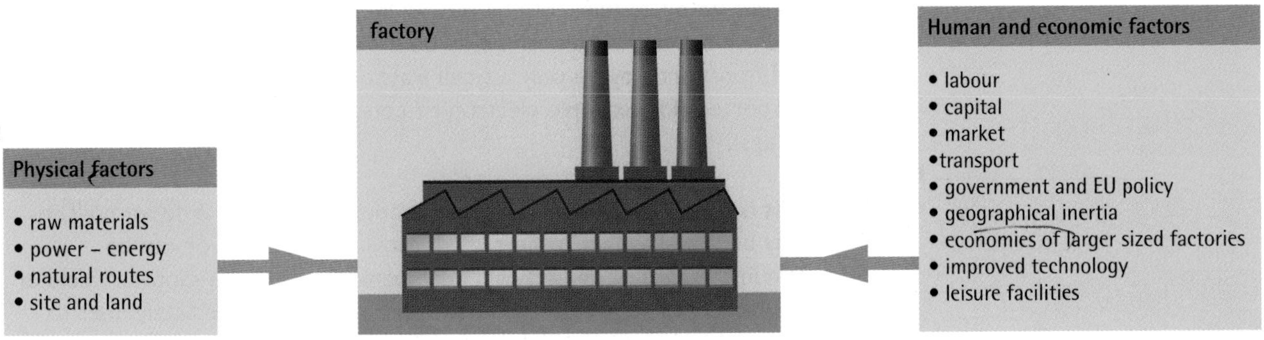

factory	Human and economic factors
	• labour
	• capital
	• market
Physical factors	•transport
	• government and EU policy
• raw materials	• geographical inertia
• power – energy	• economies of larger sized factories
• natural routes	• improved technology
• site and land	• leisure facilities

Figure 7·2 – Factors influencing location of Industry

The location of any industry depends on the interaction of several different factors.

Each of these factors can influence to a greater or lesser extent where a particular industrial unit may be sited.

Raw materials

- These are the materials from which products are made. Note that they may consist of basic materials such as coal, or semi-finished materials such as strips of steel or rolls of cotton or wool. Some industries have to be located at the source of these materials, as is the case with extractive industries. Others may have to be located very close to them so as to reduce the cost and difficulties of transport. Many of the older industries had to locate near their raw materials.

Labour supply

- All industries, to a greater or lesser extent, need labour. Modern industries however, need to consider whether labour is available and, more importantly, whether labour with appropriate skills is available. Often companies may locate in areas where older industries have declined, leaving a large unemployed labour force that needs work. Some industries, however, require less labour than was previously the case due to the introduction of technology.

Power

- In the past, power was provided by either water or steam. The need for water (to drive machinery) or coal or wood (to create heat for steam), often meant that industries had to be very close to one or both of these sources. River sites or coalfield sites were often considered to be the best places to establish industries such as heavy metal production, textiles, engineering works and food processing works.

Transport
*   Access to industries is necessary both for obtaining raw materials and for transporting the finished product to the eventual market place whether this is another industry or a shop.
*   Good access may be provided by either road, rail, water or air. Therefore, many industrial sites are located near major roads or motorways, railway lines, in river valleys or at the coast, or near major airports. The type of transport required greatly depends on the type of product being moved. Heavy bulk products such as coal, metals, wood, textiles may be moved by road or rail transport. Lighter products which are more expensive may be moved by air transport. In this case, the cost of transport may be only a small fraction of the cost of the product being transported (for example electronic / computer based products, jewellery, medical drugs).

Market
*   The market is simply the place where the product or service is delivered. The market may be very local as in the case of retailing industries, or can be world-wide in the case of multinational companies such as the motor vehicle or electronics industries. Few industries need to be located immediately next to their market.

Government and EU policy
*   Governments can attract industries to areas by offering a range of grants, subsidies, rent-free accommodation and other financial incentives to major industrial companies. Through its regional aid schemes, the EU can offer a wide variety of incentives to help to improve the economy of areas which have problems such as high unemployment, industrial decline and slow economic growth.

Industrial inertia
*   Inertia is the term used to describe the situation whereby an industry will continue to operate in an area although the original location factors may no longer be a major influence. This may happen because it could be too costly to close the industry and move it elsewhere.

Economies of larger factories / Improved technology
*   Large factories may find it convenient to locate beside each other in order to share the benefits of cost of land or reduce transport costs if trading goods with each other. Improved technology such as use of computers can allow industries such as communications / newspapers to locate in a variety of areas and have information transferred from the centre to production sites.

Key Point 4

You should be able to describe the locational factors which help in attracting foreign manufacturing industries to an area

Local and national governments can have a major influence on the location of industry.

At a national level, governments can intervene in the process of attracting industries to different parts of the country.

Measures employed include:
- Offering grants to firms to go to specified areas, e.g. areas suffering from industrial decline. Offering subsidies, perhaps to help firms construct premises, purchase machinery or pay labour costs.
- Offering assistance with labour costs by contributing to re-training schemes, paying additional premiums on salaries to attract workers.
- Offering tax incentives to companies by, for example, reducing certain company taxes for a number of years in order to encourage the company to set up business.
- Combining with local government to reduce or remove rents and rates for an agreed set period to assist in the company's early development.
- Contributing to the costs of infrastructure improvements in the area, such as new road or rail links (e.g. motorways).
- In the case of older industries, providing financial assistance to help these industries during periods of economic recession. This may allow the companies to continue trading within the areas where they were originally located.

Reasons for adopting these measures include:
- Boosting the economies of depressed areas.
- Helping to reduce the levels of unemployment within specific areas.
- Trying to assist in the process of re-industrialisation, namely by replacing older, declining industries with a newer, more modern and economically successful industrial base.
- Attempting to decentralise industry from the economically stronger areas of the country (e.g. the south east of Britain) to weaker areas such as the north east and north west where many traditional industries have declined.
- Attracting foreign investment by encouraging non-European companies to set up bases in Britain, thereby giving them the opportunity to trade within the European community. In this way both the country and the company will enjoy mutual benefits.

Industrial landscapes

Key Point 5

Using an O.S. map you should be able to describe the main features of an industrial landscape. You may also be asked to use map evidence to explain the location of industry on the map

Analysis of O.S. Maps

Many of the questions asked in the unit tests and the external examination concentrate on the interpretation of a variety of maps that contain different examples of industrial land use.

Essentiallly, these questions ask candidates:

1) to describe both the distribution and type of industries present,

2) to explain their distribution / location pattern.

The first task is therefore to correctly identify the type of industry present. The map might contain old, traditional industries, extractive industries, manufacturing and service industries, new modern light industry and industry which is transport or port related, such as shipbuilding, dockyards, warehouses, railway stockyards or aircraft industries.

The obvious problem is what to look for. Figure 7·3 illustrates three different industrial areas which could be seen on an O.S. map.

Figure 7.3 (a, b, c) – Selected industrial sites on an ordnance survey map

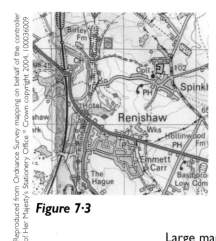

Figure 7·3

The first example shows a site of **primary industry**.

Primary industry including mining, quarrying, forestry estates and farming should be easily recognised on O.S. maps. Their location is obviously determined by the presence of the raw material being extracted and, in the case of farming, the height and shape of the land.

Occasionally there may be examples of some former extractive industry and the prefix 'dis' will be seen. This indicates a disused mine or a disused quarry and is often a good guide to the changing pattern of industry in an area.

The second example shows a site of a **manufacturing industry**. Large manufacturing industries such as iron and steelworks or engineering plants should be easily spotted by the shape of the buildings on the map as shown on Figure 7·3. Often the word 'works' will be written beside the factory along with other descriptive words such as 'aluminium'.

Power stations are also easily identified by written descriptions beside them.

Similar written descriptions may accompany 'mills' and 'distilleries'. Often large-scale factories may have their own railway line leading into the factory from the main line. Most older industries in a city will be located close to the centre of the city, perhaps surrounding the central business district.

Most will be near the main road and rail arteries leading to the centre.

Figure 7·4

Many industries may be located along one or both banks of a river. These can include port industries, docks, shipyards, warehouses, food processing plants, petrochemical plants, oil refineries and possibly even iron and steel factories.

The sites of former industries are often used as development sites for newer industrial units since the land may be cheaper and more easily obtained than in other parts of the settlement.

The third example shows the site of **modern industry**.

Modern industries will generally be found in industrial estates, either within or on the boundary of large urban areas. The words 'ind. est.' indicate their presence.

Buildings will be smaller and laid out in a more planned manner than the larger factories. Street patterns will have less of a grid iron pattern than those with the older industries and there may be easy access to a nearby motorway.

A more recent development has been the emergence of 'Science parks' and 'enterprise zones / trading estates' in many settlements. These may be named on the map and the science park may be named after a local university.

Figure 7·5

Industrial change

Key Point 6

With reference to an area you have studied, you should be able to describe and account for changes in an industrial area

Depending on the area you have studied you may refer to the following:
Many areas throughout Britain and Europe have experienced considerable change during the last 50 years.
A large number of the older industries that provided the basis for economic prosperity have declined due to a number of factors. These factors are very common and include:

- Exhaustion of raw materials such as coal, iron ore, metals etc.
- Loss of markets for products such as ships, iron and steel, textiles and engineering products. Increased competition from other areas such as developing countries, e.g. South Korea.
- Changing consumer tastes, e.g. plastics, synthetic fibres replacing natural fibres such as cotton and wool.

- Increased use of new technologies which older industries have failed to develop.
- Changes in government policies that have led to the withdrawal of financial assistance for struggling industries.
- Part of the strategy of allowing older, less profitable industries to decline included replacing them, wherever possible, with new 'sunrise' industries such as electronics and other computer-based industries.

Key Point 7

With reference to an industrial area you have studied, you should be able to refer to the factors which led to the growth of early industry; refer to any primary industry such as coal mining and explain why the area has gone into industrial decline

Case study of changing industrial area – south Wales

One area that has undergone change in its industrial landscape over the last 50 years, is south Wales. The pattern of change is well documented in a number of videos made of the area. These changes are summarised in Figure 7·6.

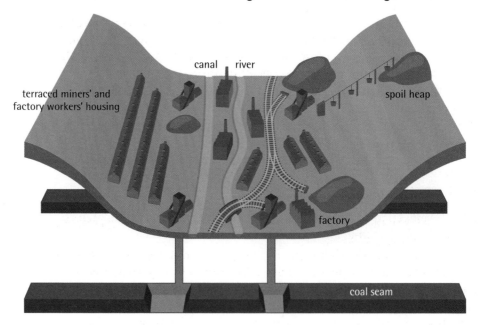

Figure 7·6 – Industrial change: south Wales in 1910

These changes in south Wales have taken place as follows:
- About 200 years ago, the period known as the Industrial Revolution was taking place in Britain. This period saw the emergence of most of Britain's traditional industries including coal-mining, iron and steel manufacture, shipbuilding, textile production and heavy engineering.

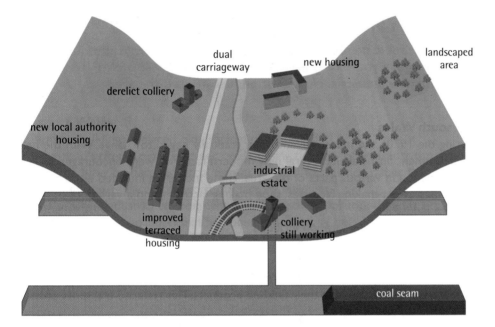

Figure 7·6 – Industrial change: south Wales in 1985

- South Wales was an ideal place to develop most of these industries as the area had the main raw materials needed for the growth of these industries namely, coal, iron ore and limestone. These three rocks were found in abundance in the valleys of south Wales. With the development of the iron and steel industry, a basic market was provided for coal mining. The growth of these industries attracted many people from rural areas to work in these factories and coal mines.

- Coal and steel were also exported abroad to many of the countries of the British Empire including, for example, India. Other industrial developments, such as the railways, provided a further market for coal and steel. Developments of railways across parts of the Empire increased the demand for Welsh steel. In effect, the three main factors responsible for the growth of industry in this area were availability of raw materials, the demand from a home and foreign market, and a plentiful supply of labour.

- During the 1950s, the situation began to change. The raw materials, which were once in plentiful supply, began to run out. Mines had to be dug much deeper to get at the coal seams and this led to increased costs. Other materials such as iron ore had to be imported, again increasing production costs.

- The most important blow, however, was the decline in the market for the products of the traditional industries. By the 1950s, the British Empire no longer existed and many of the countries which had supplied a market began to develop their own industries.

- This market decline led to the decline of the industrial base of south Wales. Mines and steelworks closed at an alarming rate. This inevitably led to many job losses.

- Not surprisingly, many unemployed people moved away in search of work elsewhere, for example to the south east of England. The landscape was littered with closed factories and closed mines.

Sample answer – 2(a)

South Wales was once a major coal mining and steel works area ✓. These have declined for several reasons.

The coal seams were becoming thinner ✓ so making it too expensive to run the mines ✓. Cheaper raw materials were coming in ✓ from the vast open cast mines of Australia ✓ and the USA. The decline of the British Empire meant that the markets for British coal and steel were no longer there ✓.

The finished products, i.e. ships, trains were now being produced for much lower costs in countries such as Japan and Taiwan ✓.

There was a general shift in the market. Manufacturing and production line work rendered traditional industries obsolete ✓.

Comments and marks obtained – 2(a)

The answer makes very good references to the main factors responsible for the decline of the industries within the named area including the seams becoming thinner and more expensive to mine, the availability of cheaper raw materials from named areas, the finished products being produced cheaper, again in appropriate, named areas.

All of these points were sufficient to gain a total of $8 \times \frac{1}{2}$ marks giving a total of 4 out of 5 marks for part (a).

Sample answer – 2(b)

As the industries in South Wales declined, the area was hit by many problems. Large numbers of men were made unemployed ✓ and their families suffered badly. The area was hit by widespread depression ✓.

The economy was hit badly as there were no new industries to replace the coal and steel works.

The area was also scarred by the large buildings of the works ✓ as well as the large slag heaps left by the coal mines ✓.

New industries were not initially attracted to the area so it became very difficult for the population. to find work ✓. Large railway sidings and lines also scarred the land ✓.

The derelict buildings were hazardous and nobody could afford to remove them ✓.

Comments and marks obtained – 2(b)

The impact of the changes on the area are fairly well discussed. Appropriate references to unemployment, widespread depression, scarring of the landscape by derelict buildings, slag heaps and railway sidings, the lack of attraction of new industry to the area making it difficult to find work and the cost of removal of older buildings all obtained a total of $7 \times \frac{1}{2}$ marks for a total of $3\frac{1}{2}$ out of 4.

As in part (a), there were statements that simply repeated points already made, such as 'the economy being badly hit' that essentially repeated the point made about the widespread depression. These repetitions did not achieve any further marks.

Taken together, parts (a) and (b) obtained a total of $7\frac{1}{2}$ marks out of a possible 9.

Marking instructions

Question 1

Answers to both parts of this question will obviously depend upon the candidate's choice of 'named industrial concentration'.

Answers should be assessed out of 9 with up to 5 marks for either part, awarding a $\frac{1}{2}$ mark for each relevant point.

Usually a maximum of 7 marks is available if answers do not refer to a specific area.

1(a) Answers should be able to make reasonably detailed and authentic references to the importance of physical factors such as –

- proximity to raw materials such as coal, iron ore and limestone (for example, in south Wales);
- water power giving way to steam power, noting the link with coal;
- the relative ease of extracting coal near the surface and thick seams in the south Wales coal-field valleys in the early years of the industry;
- the importance of water transport (canals and barges on the Rhine in the case of the Ruhr); and the close proximity to the coast for export through the ports, (for example, Cardiff).

1(b) Answers should comment (with reference to the chosen area) on human and economic influences such as –

- the need to be close to motorway links for easy import / export of components and finished products;
- the influence of government and EU incentives in attracting new industries in depressed areas;
- the importance of proximity to a large market;
- the importance of a well trained workforce;
- the impact of geographical inertia in maintaining the existence of some older industry;
- the significance of the presence of foreign-owned companies setting up in the area to gain access to European market; the advantages of being close to universities and colleges for research and development and highly skilled personnel;
- the development of tourism using former industrial sites, e.g. coal mines.

Question 2

2 (a) Assess out of 5 with each relevant point awarded a $\frac{1}{2}$ mark.
Candidates could refer to:

- overseas competition in the manufacturing industry;
- cheaper to import raw materials;
- local supplies of raw materials running out or becoming less economic to mine;
- old infrastructure;
- old fashioned factories;
- world demand for heavy industrial products in decline.

2 (b) Assess out of 4 with a maximum of 3 for environmental or social consequences.

Environmental consequences could include:

- Air and river pollution
- pit bings, slag heaps etc;
- derelict buildings;
- failing infrastructure;
- poor quality housing.

Social consequences could include:

- High unemployment;
- out-migration;
- high levels of ill health;
- domino effect on smaller industries, shops etc.
- rising crime rates;
- vandalism of older property.

GLOSSARY OF ASSOCIATED TERMS

Brownfield site: A site that was once developed but has now been abandoned, e.g. a derelict area in a city.

Business parks: Areas which have become industrial estates with businesses which may sell products or provide services directly to the public.

Dereliction and decay: This refers to abandoned buildings (perhaps mines, offices or industries) which have resulted from closures; often they become a source of visual pollution if they are not demolished.

Diversification: This is the process whereby an economic enterprise such as a farm takes on a range of additional activities to increase profits for example, renting land for golf courses, caravan sites, paint ball enterprises, quad biking.

Economic: Relating to financial developments.

Economic effects: The financial impact of change on, for example, employment, incomes, running costs, building costs and costs to the local community.

Environmental consequences: The effects of change on the physical and human environments, for example changing land use, improvements and bad effects on the environment such as increased pollution, changes to the population caused by people moving to or from areas as a result of change such as industrial closures or new industry being built.

Enterprise zone: An area which receives government assistance to attract new industry and create new employment opportunity.

Extractive Industry: Primary industry which takes raw materials from the ground, e.g. mining, quarrying, fishing, forestry.

Greenfield site: Land which has not been previously used for industry or any other buildings.

Heavy Industry: Industry which produces heavy bulk materials, e.g. iron and steel, textiles, shipbuilding.

High-tech industry: Industry which uses the latest technology to produce goods and services.

Industrial decline: This happens when for various reasons industries in an area have to close. This has largely involved large traditional, heavy industry such as mining, iron and steel making, textiles and shipbuilding.

Industrial estate: An area set aside for modern, light industrial units, often located on the outskirts of towns / cities where land is available and the area is served by a good communication system, e.g. motorways.

Industrial growth: This happens when an industry increases its output, number of workers and profits and usually has a positive effect on the local community.

Industrial inertia: This occurs when an industry remains in an area long after the original location factors no longer apply.

Light industry: Industries which manufacture small, light bulk products, e.g. window frames, kitchen appliances.

Manufacturing industry: Industries which make a variety of products that are either finished or semi-finished.

Multiplier effect: This is the wider, positive effect of change on other activities such as other industries, settlements or rural activities. This effect occurs where investment of capital (or the location of a company) in an area pumps prices in the local economy, hopefully encouraging other businesses to set up in that area.

Primary industry: Industries which are based on extracting raw materials such as coal, ores, farm produce and forests.

Reverse Multiplier effect: This is the wider, negative effect of change on other activities such as other industries, settlements or rural activities. For example, when a major industry closes this may cause local shops and other business to close since people made unemployed have less money to spend and may move elsewhere to seek new work.

Science parks: These are industrial areas which are closely connected to technological institutions and universities and are often involved in producing high technology products. They have often helped to replace declining industries and have offered new job opportunities to workers from closed industries following retraining schemes.

Service industry: Also referred to as 'tertiary' industries which provide services such as retailing, wholesaling, transport, legal, administrative and trades for communities.

Sunrise industries: Term used to describe new modern highly technological industries such as electronics. These industries are normally growing and gradually replacing older, declining industries.

URBAN

> ### Key Point I
> You should know the main factors that can affect the site of a town or city. You should refer to a case study of a named developed world city

The 'site' of a settlement is the actual land on which the original settlement was built. Figure 8·1 shows a number of idealised sites for settlements.

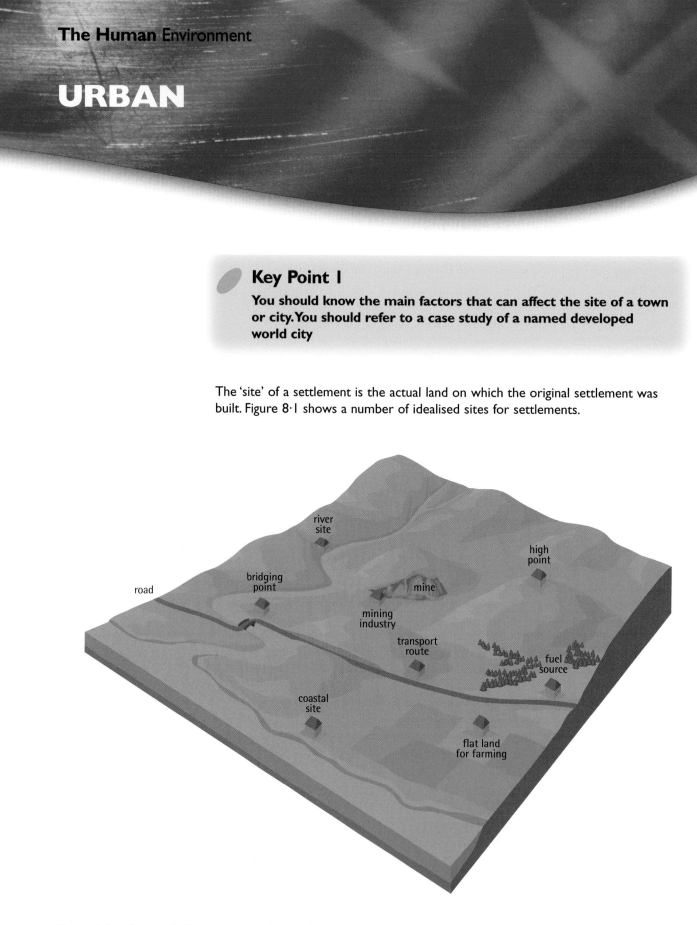

Figure 8·1 – Factors influencing a settlement's location

Influential site factors

*   A site which is **near to a supply of fresh water**. This usually means choosing a site in part of a river valley. Other freshwater sites would include sites near a source of underground water which could be obtained from a well and sites near a spring line.
*   A site which provides **flat land for building on** and room for expansion as the settlement grows.
*   Areas which have **good, fertile soils** will be attractive for settlement.
*   Early settlements were often built **close to a source of fuel** such as a forest or woodland area.
*   Sites on areas of **dry firm land**. This was important in areas where the ground consisted largely of marshland or fenland. The settlements were built on islands of dry land and have since been referred to as *'dry point'* sites.
*   Sites which offered **good defence against potential enemies** such as a high point for building a castle or fortress were also selected. If these sites also commanded a strategic position – for example overlooking major routes – this offered an added advantage.
*   Some sites were chosen because they were at the **centre of major routes** or perhaps lay in a gap between upland and lowland areas. These sites are known as *'gap'* sites.
*   The **lowest point at which a river could be crossed** was often chosen. These sites offered good opportunities for the development of trade. These sites are called *'lowest bridging points'*.
*   With the development of industry and the need for raw materials, areas which had **raw materials** such as coal, iron ore and other minerals were chosen for the development of mining centres.
*   Coastal areas with **access to the sea** would afford opportunities for both fishing and transport by sea.

Clearly more than one factor can influence the site of a settlement. Sites which had a combination of advantages of being close to water, with flat land, fertile soils and close to the lowest bridging point of a river were very popular for early settlers.

Identifying sites factors from O.S. map evidence

When trying to identify the original factors which influenced the site of a present day settlement using an Ordnance Survey map, refer to the following evidence.

*   Contour lines (or lack of them) will indicate the flatness or steepness of the land. Nearness to a water source such as a river or stream can clearly be seen.
*   The accessibility of the original site will also be fairly evident from the number of roads in the area.
*   If the site is on the meander of a river, this may have offered protection from potential attack. Similarly, fortifications on high land will indicate the past influence of defence as an important factor.
*   Mines or quarries (sometimes currently disused) will indicate the past or current presence of raw materials.

Key Point 4

You should be able to describe and account for the location of functional zones within a town or city, from the CBD to the suburbs

In your answer you could refer to models of settlement structure with which you should already be familiar. A model is simply a way of showing what the ideal structure of a settlement would be under idealised conditions.

The urban models which are most often referred to include:

a)   The Concentric city model
b)   The Sector model
c)   The Multiple nuclei model

Figure 8·2 (a) (b) (c) – Models of urban structure

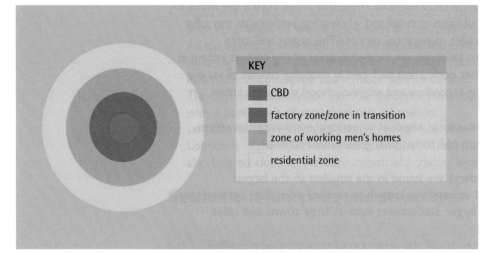

KEY

CBD

factory zone/zone in transition

zone of working men's homes

residential zone

All of these models contain areas known as functional zones. These are areas where one particular function dominates, e.g. retailing / commercial, industry or different types of housing.

Figure 8·2 (a) – Concentric city model

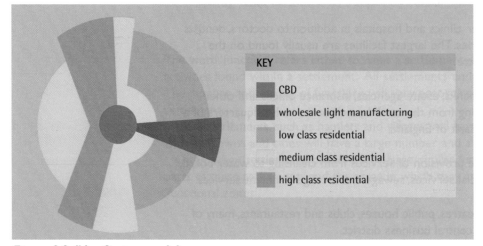

KEY

CBD

wholesale light manufacturing

low class residential

medium class residential

high class residential

Each of these zones can be identified on an O.S. map, usually from the pattern of communications: road / rail lines usually converge on the CBD; streets in low-cost housing areas are usually arranged in a grid iron pattern compared with curvilinear street patterns and cul-de-sacs in medium- to higher-cost housing areas.

Figure 8·2 (b) – Sector model

On O.S. maps, large blocks indicate tenements and areas with named types of industry (for example works or industrial estates) can easily be identified. The presence of specific functions, such as bus and railway terminals within the CBD, can also be noted on the ordnance survey map.

The actual structure and location of each zone will vary from city to city and town to town.

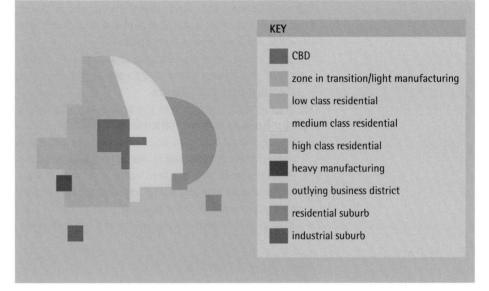

KEY

- CBD
- zone in transition/light manufacturing
- low class residential
- medium class residential
- high class residential
- heavy manufacturing
- outlying business district
- residential suburb
- industrial suburb

Figure 8·2 (c) – Multiple nuclei model

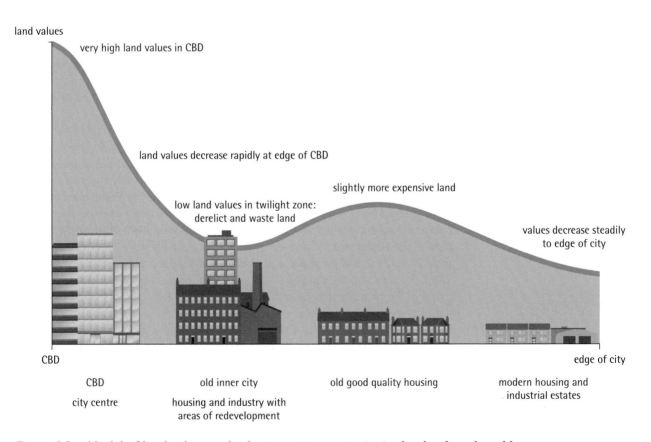

land values

very high land values in CBD

land values decrease rapidly at edge of CBD

slightly more expensive land

low land values in twilight zone: derelict and waste land

values decrease steadily to edge of city

| CBD | | edge of city |

| CBD | old inner city | old good quality housing | modern housing and industrial estates |
| city centre | housing and industry with areas of redevelopment | | |

Figure 8·3 – Model of land values and urban zones across a city in the developed world

Figure 8·3 shows that land values are highest at the city centre (CBD) due to the area being the most accessible and the fact that it contains the functions which can compete for the highest land prices.

- Land values begin to decrease as one moves further away from the centre, although industry can afford to pay higher rents / prices for land immediately at the edge of the city centre.
- Prices rapidly decrease in the area known as the twilight zone, an area of low-cost housing – mainly tenements.
- Further away from the poor environments of these areas, land values begin to rise and this is reflected in the better quality housing found in the suburbs.
- At the edge of the city, land values decrease once again and often land is used for industrial estates, out of town shopping centres, council house estates and areas of private housing estates.
- You should refer to these points and use examples of zones from a named city.

Key Point 5

You should be able to identify the CBD of a settlement on an ordnance survey map, giving map evidence to support your choice. You should also be able to compare two CBDs, referring to their location and land use

If you are asked to identify the CBD, there are certain features you should look for on the map.

- As most maps show, the main roads converge on this area. You would refer to this and identify roads by name if possible.
- You would also look for buildings such as, train and bus stations, town halls, museums, information centres, perhaps colleges and other large further education establishments, large churches, possibly even cathedrals, large blocks of buildings which could be shopping malls, car parks and possibly theatres.
- It is unlikely that there would be much evidence of industry, either in estates or large works. There would also be little evidence of housing. However the street patterns may show small narrow streets at the very centre indicating the oldest part of the settlement. Whenever these features are identified, grid references of their location should be given to support identification.
- The CBD may also be identified in terms of its location in that most would be found in the most central point of the city and certainly the part of the city which is the most accessible.
- There may be some streets which have different shapes such as small cul-de-sacs and curves. These streets may contain large terraced houses which have been converted to offices.
- This has happened in, for example, Edinburgh and Glasgow.

Comparison of two CBDs would refer to aspects such as

- location within the settlmement
- accessibility with reference to roads, railways, bus and train stations
- the general size of the areas
- types of zones close by, e.g. industry or housing
- perhaps comment on the presence of individual functions such as tourist information centres, churches etc.

Key Point 6

You should be able to describe the site and account for the location of particular zones within a town

1. The core area – Central Business District

- The site of this area is often but not always in the centre of the settlement and it should be the most accessible point, indicated by the convergence of all major transport routes, both road and rail.
- Due to this highly accessible position, it is the area where most services would like to locate so as to gain maximum access to their customers.
- Functions such as retailing, wholesaling, offices, services, public administration, entertainment transport terminals, art centres are all located here.
- This is also the area where land prices are most expensive and only those functions which can afford the relatively high cost of this land can compete for space.

2. The Industrial zone

- Normally the sites of industrial areas have certain common features such as flat land and accessibility in terms of roads, rivers, canals and possibly motorways. The older industrial areas are normally located close to the CBD.
- This zone should contain a range of manufacturing industries including, for example, textiles, engineering and food-processing.
- This zone will contain large blocks of buildings, often with the name '*works*' beside them. These may also be found along the side of roads and railway lines with several of the largest industries having small railway tracks leading from the main line into the works. If there is a river, there will be various industrial units along the banks, including warehouses, docks, perhaps shipbuilding, oil refineries and power stations. Various industrial areas may be found in a variety of locations throughout the settlement.
- Newer industrial areas may be seen either on the outskirts – in the area known as the '*rural-urban fringe*' – in industrial estates or nearer the city centre in redeveloped sites of former older industries. Land values are lower in these areas, although the sites must be located near major route networks (motorways) for access for raw materials and finished products. Industries will be modern and contained in newer buildings with wider streets, perhaps lined with trees.
- The buildings in areas of new industry will be made up of smaller units than the large factories in the older zone.
- Instead of textile factories, engineering works or iron and steel works typical of the older zone, new industries will be based on perhaps electronics, small-scale manufacturing such as clothes making, window manufacturers and. stationery supplies.

3. Area of low-cost housing

This zone contains mainly less expensive, often older houses. Since it is closest to the industrial zone, the houses would have been used primarily to house the workers of the industries in zone 2.

4. Area of medium-cost housing

As some people in the settlement became more affluent they found that they could afford to move further away from the centre into areas where the problems of zone 3 (traffic congestion / pollution) were reduced. Housing in this zone is of a better quality, less densely built with a better layout of streets, more garden areas, less traffic and less pollution. This is clearly identifiable on O.S. maps.

5. Area of high-cost housing

As more of the population could afford to move even further away from the city centre and the cost of travel reduced, a further zone of housing emerged. This area consists of low density, high cost housing such as bungalows detached and semi-detached houses. These are most likely to be located on the periphery of major settlements. All of the zones grow outwards from the centre of the city.

Key Point 7

You should be able to describe and contrast the features of urban zones within a town or city and explain why the environments of particular zones are so different

Housing

- Different housing areas can be identified by their street patterns.
- Low-cost housing areas have houses which were built in a grid iron pattern, often with small narrow streets. They will be situated very close to the older industrial areas, to allow workers quick and easy access to their place of employment.
- The environments of older low-cost housing areas are not very pleasant. The housing will almost certainly consist of tenements, which are high density housing.
- Many of these tenements may be showing signs of age and the effects of years of pollution from nearby factories. Some cities have demolished many of the older tenements and have replaced them with newer flats and very often high rise flats.
- Many people have also been re-housed in schemes built on the boundary of cities. These are recognisable by their layout, which is often very similar to the high density older tenement areas of the inner city.
- Higher cost housing may be recognised from street patterns of curvilinear streets, cul-de-sacs and gardens. They will be areas of low density housing with wider, sometimes tree-lined, streets. Houses may consist of tenements, terraces, semi-detached and detached buidldings.
- The overall environment will be much more pleasant with less traffic and less pollution than in the inner city areas.
- There may be a wide range of functions such as schools, small shopping centres, recreational areas and open space, to a much greater extent than the inner city.

Key Point 8

You should be able to give map evidence to suggest the likely function of a settlement, e.g. resort or mining towns

Although most settlements offer a variety of functions, depending on size, occasionally one function may tend to dominate within particular settlements. This has led to descriptions of towns such as *mining towns*, *textile towns*, *ports*, *resorts*, *university towns*, *cathedral towns*, *market towns* and *garrison towns*.

These are just a few examples of the many settlements which have one dominant function. In addition to these there are other towns which are classified as '*dormitory*' settlements. These are settlements located on the outskirts of major towns and cities.

The majority of people who reside in these settlements do not work in the place where they live. They actually commute on a daily basis to work elsewhere, usually in the nearest large town or city.

Finally there are a group of settlements known as '*New Towns*'. These are settlements which have been planned and built since the 1950s and have their own town councils, for example East Kilbride in Scotland and Crawley in England.

Map evidence

The kind of map evidence you would present would depend on the type of town identified.

For example resorts would have perhaps a pier, conference centre, rail and bus terminals, recreational facilities etc. You would see evidence of collieries / disused mines in mining towns and large scale industrial areas within industrial / manufacturing towns.

Key Point 9

For a named city in the developed world you should be able to describe and account for the pattern of land uses within the CBD

Case study – Glasgow

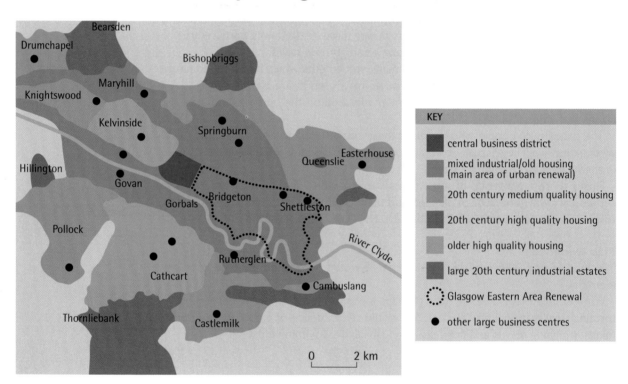

Figure 8·4 – Zones in Glasgow

- The Central Business District of Glasgow (Zone 1) is located on the northern edge of the River Clyde stretching a distance of approximately 4 kilometres west to east and 2.5 kilometres north from the river.
- This area contains all of the functions you would expect to find in any Central Business District, including department stores, a wide range of shops of various sizes, entertainment, wholesale businesses, restaurants, offices and other service industries, train and bus and subway stations and several large undercover shopping centres which is a feature of many redeveloped Central Business Districts.
- Unlike some cities, it also contains features such as public parks, cathedrals and other churches.
- The layout of the CBD is a grid iron pattern due to intensive town planning. This planning was based around the area known as the Merchant City which lies within the eastern sector of the CBD.
- The River Clyde acts as a barrier to further development of the CBD to the south.

Urban change

> ### Key Point 10
>
> **Referring to a named city in the developed world you should describe and account for changes which have occurred both within the CBD and inner city, explaining why they were necessary and comment on their relative success**

Change in the Central Business District of Glasgow

- Some of the greatest changes that have happened to cities in recent years have occurred in the Central Business Districts. As populations declined in cities, so many shops found their trade being seriously affected. Without trade to keep profits at a reasonable level, many shops and other services were no longer able to remain in business. Closures and 'For Sale' signs have been commonplace in many town centres for some years.
- Many large department stores especially have found it hard to remain open as independent units. Many have been replaced by the 'franchise' type of operation, e.g. Debenhams. These shops offer floor space to various retailers such as 'Principles' for an agreed rent. This offsets costs and allows the stores to remain in business.
- Other changes have included the building of undercover shopping arcades such as the Princess Arcade, the St. Enoch's centre and Buchanan Galleries where shoppers can shop in much greater comfort. Most large cities have centres such as these. An additional advantage is that these also provide essential parking facilities for their customers.
- Pedestrian zones, which do not permit through-traffic during business hours, are also popular and help to attract custom back to the older shopping areas.

Reasons for change

- Measures such as these have changed the style and character of city centre shopping areas and have helped them to compete against out-of-town shopping and business complexes. These have greatly increased in number and are a threat to the older centres. They have added advantages such as free transport and parking services plus a wide range of services catering for the needs of families. They are often combined with other services such as cinemas, restaurants and other recreational facilities.
- Many centres such as the Gyle Centre located on the Western outskirts of Edinburgh, the Metro Centre on the edge of Newcastle and, most recently, the Braehead centre between Glasgow and Paisley are typical examples of this type of new centre.
- New road schemes, redeveloped and redesigned buildings, which are used for offices, housing projects or conference centres are designed to make Glasgow's CBD more accessible, maximise building space and attract more custom to the city centres.
- Other changes in the city's CBD have included the renovation of old buildings such as the GPO into high cost flats to attract people back into the city; changes to road systems to ease traffic congestion; closure of several shops due to high rates and lost customers; conversion of terraced housing to office premises to increase business.

Change in the inner city area of Glasgow
- The CBD is surrounded by a zone of industry which includes a variety of different manufacturing units. Many of these have replaced older industries such as heavy engineering works and textile factories.
- It is more common to see modern prefabricated buildings in estates rather than large bleak factories although some still exist in other parts of the city.
- The city is dissected by the River Clyde which flows in an east / west direction through the city. Along the banks of the river, from the CBD to the western edge of the city, are the remnants of Glasgow's port industries including warehouses, food processing industries, docks, harbours and shipyards.
- Overlying this pattern is the very important influence of planning. This planning influence was effective from an early stage of Glasgow's development. Next to the low-cost area there are areas of medium- to higher-cost housing.
- The street pattern is quite different from the low-cost housing. Cul-de-sacs and curvilinear street patterns have reached the rigid blocks of the grid iron pattern. Streets are wider, housing is much less dense, with smaller units often with garden areas. The streets also have some trees to improve the look of the area.
- Altogether, the environment is much better and much more pleasant than it had been previously. There are additional facilities such as churches, schools, recreational centres and park areas. Housing consists of a mixture of red sandstone tenements, red and grey sandstone terraced and semi-detached houses.

Key Point 11

You should be able to describe impact of new developments, in particular urban zones and be able to discuss any problems resulting from changes

Your answer might refer to changes to work, shopping and housing patterns. You might also refer to old dilapidated factory sites that have been demolished in many cities and have been replaced by new trading estates. The environments of these areas have been transformed thoroughly.

Problems
- These new estates do not always employ as many people as the industries which they replaced and unemployment often remains a problem.
- Many people now work from home using the advantage of technology. This new industry has helped to change the patterns of journeys to work throughout city areas. Many people who spent a large proportion of their working day travelling from home to work or between workplaces can now handle most of their work through the use of computers.
- This has made a considerable difference to their choice of residence. The impact of this trend on cities has still to be determined.
- One other problem is evident, namely, the loss of population which moved to countryside areas. This is a problem due to the reduction of trade in the city.
- The increase in demand for housing in the rural-urban fringe or greenbelt area will obviously have an effect the environment of these areas. However, this might be offset by the reduction of traffic and all the problems associated with this.

- Changes to transport newworks in and around the CBD have affected many cities, e.g. introduction of new one way systems, bus lanes and restricted parking in helping to ease traffic congestion.
- Some businesses on major routes have suffered through lack of customers because drivers can no longer park on main roads. Other businesses have suffered through competition with out of town shopping centres.
- Rengeneration schemes in some inner city housing areas have radically changed the quality of housing and the local environment of many housing zones in cities.
- Older properties have been demolished and replaced with new housing. This has included demolishing high rise flats built during the 1960s which caused great problems for residents, particularly young families and elderly people.
- Many families and older communities have been broken up and redistributed to areas throughout the city and have lost a sense of community spirit and security.

GEOGRAPHICAL METHODS AND TECHNIQUES

Key Point 12

You should be able to describe and analyse land use maps, transects and survey data, e.g. land-use maps from CBD to suburbs, and sphere of influence studies

Most techniques involved with urban geography attempt to identify and explain patterns of land use and change in urban areas.

Some of the analysis will be based on ordnance survey maps and will involve identifying some of the patterns discussed earlier in this chapter.

- Street patterns, the size and shape of buildings and identifying certain types of buildings from the key provided should help you to identify different zones within an urban area.
- You can use these features to draw comparisons between areas, for example, different housing zones, the CBD and the suburbs and so on.
- Your explanation of these patterns can be based on your knowledge of functional zones within a city, as discussed earlier.
- You can refer to transport patterns, road, rail and water networks to explain the location of service areas and industrial areas.

You may be presented with an actual land-use map based on a survey carried out in an urban area. The land use may be divided into categories such as **R**esidential, **I**ndustrial, **C**ommercial, **E**ntertainment, **P**ublic buildings, **O**ffices and **T**ransport (**RICEPOTS**). You can analyse these maps by noting the most important land uses, the proximity of certain land uses to each other and why certain land uses are present.

The technique of land-use mapping using **RICEPOTS** as a basis for annotating the land use map, (see above categories) is often used to classify certain land uses.

Often, instead of providing a land-use map of a whole area, a sample survey, based on a transect, (a line drawn through the urban area, for example along a main road) noting the land uses present is very used.

- Different categories of land use can be analysed to determine if a pattern exists. For example, certain land uses may predominate near the city centre whilst others may predominate at regular intervals away from the centre towards the edge of the city.
- Your knowledge of urban models and urban zones should help you to explain the pattern and the land uses within certain zones identified on your map.
- In the section on rural settlement we noted how the service function can affect the distribution pattern of settlements in areas where commercial farming occurs.
- Factors such as relief and transport greatly influence the pattern bringing about a regular distribution of the settlements.
- This allows each settlement, regardless of its size, to serve customers within a specific area. The shape and size of that area is largely determined by the number of services on offer.
- These service areas are known as the settlement's *sphere of influence.*

Sphere of influence

One geographical technique you should know is 'how to determine the size and shape of a settlement's sphere of influence'. There are several ways of doing this.
- First a survey of consumers shopping at a store or shopping area could be carried out using a questionnaire which is aimed at finding out where they live and how often they shop at that location.
- Second, interviews with businesses (such as a garage or department store which offer a service to customers over a specific area) can provide information on the area which they serve or to which they deliver goods.
- Third, the circulation area of a local or city newspaper will give a good indication of the area served by that settlement.
- From this information, maps can be drawn to show the extent of the service area.
- When these maps are drawn, they should indicate that the larger the service centre, the greater the area that they serve, i.e. their sphere of influence.

Key Point 13

You should be able to annotate field sketches and photographs of urban areas and comment on the accuracy of statements describing urban patterns on maps and diagrams

- Annotating field sketches and photographs is also an important technique for analysing and explaining patterns of land use within urban areas. The labels should be detailed and point out significant features of different buildings such as quality, problems, size and type.
- You can base comparisons of different areas or the same area in two different periods of time on these characteristics.
- Some explanation may be added to your answer by referring to the general changes which have taken place in urban areas, e.g. changes to the CBD or inner city areas.

SAMPLE QUESTIONS, ANSWERS, COMMENTS AND MARKING INSTRUCTIONS

Question 1

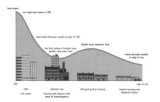

Reference Diagram Q1 –
Model of land use zones across
a city in the developed world

Study Reference Diagram Q1
Reference Diagram Q1 – Model of land use zones across a city in the Developed world (See Figure 8·3 on page 151)
Referring to a named city in the Developed World which you have studied,

(a) describe and account for the likely land uses to be observed in Zone A, and

5 marks

(b) suggest why Zone B may have experienced considerable change in the last 30–40 years.

4 marks

(9 marks)

Sample answer – 1(a)

✓ denotes correct point

> Likely land uses to be found in the CBD of Glasgow are mainly service industries ✓, e.g. shops, entertainment like cinemas, concert halls ✓. Large offices are found here because of the easy accessibility ✓. Many roads and railway lines meet in the CBD ✓. Large department stores with big names are found here, e.g. Marks and Spencers, Debenhams ✓. Bid rents are very high in the CBD ✓ because land is very desirable ✓. There are many high rise buildings ✓ because they do not take up space on the ground. There is not much space, no parks ✓, it is a built up area.

Comments and marks obtained – 1(a)

This is a good answer which contains correct descriptions of land uses within a named city, with plenty of examples of the types of land uses mentioned. Although several examples are given, only one $\frac{1}{2}$ mark is given for each list. The answer also contains explanatory points as to why certain functions are there, e.g. 'accessibility' and 'bid rents' and 'lack of space'. These comments gave three relevant points on explanation and therefore $3 \times \frac{1}{2}$ marks.

Overall the answer was good enough to obtain $9 \times \frac{1}{2}$ which is $4\frac{1}{2}$ out of 5 marks (3 out of 3 for description and $1\frac{1}{2}$ out of 2 for explanation).

Sample answer – 1(b)

> Zone B has changed because of industry. Industry declined and new more modern industry moved out to new industrial estates on the outskirts of the city ✓, e.g. Hillington ✓. New housing schemes were also built on the outskirts ✓, e.g. Castlemilk and Easterhouse ✓ so people moved away. The invention of New Towns also got people's attention. There was housing and employment there ✓, e.g. Irvine, East Kilbride, Glenrothes ✓. In zone B, tenements were found. These have been rehabilitated by the GEAR project ✓ (Glasgow Eastern Area Renewal). The old tenements were refurbished inside and out and 2 houses have been knocked into 1 to enlarge living space ✓.

Comments and marks obtained – 1(b)

The answer obtained marks for references to the changes to zone B, including industrial change, movement of population to outer areas and the comments on the rehabilitation projects with named examples.

No marks were obtained by naming the outer city housing schemes. The comments on the New Towns were irrelevant to the answer since they did not refer directly to the changes within zone B, and therefore did not obtain any further marks. The final comments on the refurbishment of older housing was worth an additional mark.

In total the answer obtained $8 \times \frac{1}{2}$ marks and a total of 4 out of 4.

Overall parts (a) and (b) gave a total of 8 out of a possible 9 marks.

Question 2

Study OS map extract Brighton on page 164.

(a) 'Brighton was the earliest coastal town to grow as a resort and has spread along the coast to Portslade and also to the east and inland'. Give map evidence to show that Brighton is a tourist resort.

3 marks

(b) Study areas A and B which represent different stages in the growth of Brighton.

For each area describe

(i) the site

(ii) the urban landscape.

6 marks

Sample answer – 2(a)

It is obvious that Brighton is a tourist resort for a number of reasons. Firstly there are a number of tourist information centres ✓ (e.g. 2804) ✓. There are also many attractions which can be visited like the museums ✓ (3104) and also the Royal Pavilion (3104). The beach would be a popular attraction with an aquarium and the Palace Pier ✓ (3103) and a leisure centre further up the coast ✓ (2804). There are campsites, caravan parks and picnic sites all around the outskirts ✓ with easy access to parking areas and roads back into town ✓. There are a lot of facilities that are good for a day out like the many nature trails, the golf courses (3207) or even the race course ✓ (3305).

Comments and marks obtained – 2(a)

This answer contains more than sufficient correct detail including relevant grid references to obtain full marks. The answer is well written and avoids simply listing the main features.

The answer therefore gains $8 \times \frac{1}{2}$ marks giving a total of 4 but only 3 marks are available therefore it gains 3 out of 3 marks.

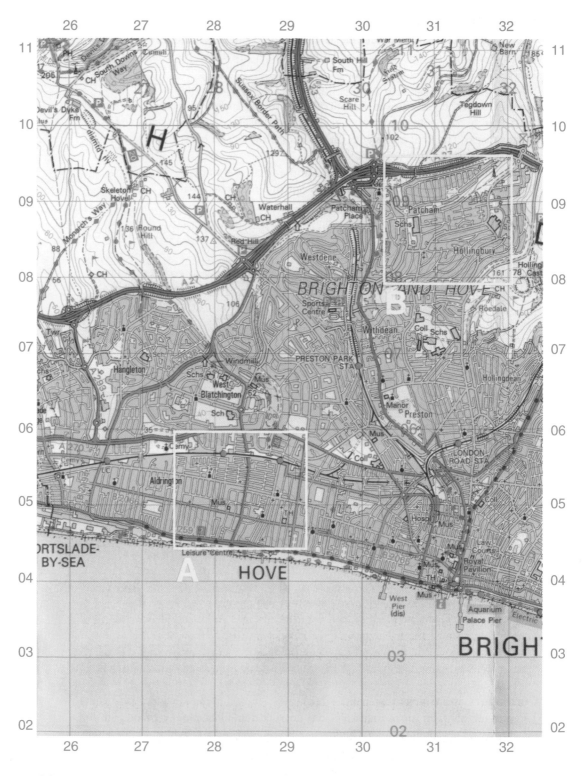

OS map extract – Brighton

Sample answer – 2(b)

> Area A is obviously the old inner city due to the grid iron street pattern ✓. The land is very flat which is obviously why they built there in the first place ✓ and there are main roads surrounding the area making it very accessible ✓. The buildings will be tenements which probably have four floors or they will be rows of terraced housing ✓. The workers from the old industries would stay there because it is in easy walking distance ✓ of the CBD.
> Area B is the modern suburban housing estate because it is on the outskirts and the streets are very irregular ✓. This is because there will be a lot o children here so the cars have to be slowed down somehow. There will probably be speed bumps and very tight corners. The houses are likely to be detached or semi-detached housing ✓ with a garage or a reasonable sized garden because the land is cheap ✓. There are roads leading back into town making the area accessible ✓. There is what looks to be an industrial estate to the south where the residents would work ✓ and there are a number of schools ✓ and the University of Sussex nearby also.

Comments and marks obtained – 2(b)

The first part of the answer obtained $2\frac{1}{2}$ marks for references to the inner city, grid iron pattern, flat land, main roads and the rows of terraced houses. The final part did not receive any marks since the reference to the workers is irrelevant. The second part of the answer obtained 3 marks for references to the modern housing estate, on the outskirts with irregular shaped streets, the semi-detached housing and the final reference to the number of schools. The explanation relating to the street patterns and safety for children etc., cheap land, roads leading to town and the industrial estate did not obtain any further marks again because of these statements being irrelevant.

The answer was good enough to obtain a total of $11 \times \frac{1}{2}$ marks which gave $5\frac{1}{2}$ out of 6 marks. Both parts together therefore obtained a total of $8\frac{1}{2}$ marks out of a possible 9 marks.

Marking instructions

Question 1

1(a) Assess description / explanation. If there are no examples from a named city, mark the total out of 4. Award a $\frac{1}{2}$ mark for each relevant point.

Description could include
- Major shopping areas with department stores;
- smaller shops servicing the working population in the CBD;
- higher order shops, (specialist shops such as electrical goods, menswear chain retailers, Chemists)
- Financial sector outlets including, banks insurance offices estate agents and building societies
- Entertainment services (cinemas, theatres, pubs restaurants, clubs etc.)
- Administration including public offices, council offices, main police offices
- Transport services including major rail and bus stations
- High cost residential apartments (perhaps refurbished buildings)

Explanation might include:
- High cost of land which only certain businesses can afford rents / leases.
- Dependent upon high accessibility, therefore major transport terminals;
- Need for access for large numbers of consumers and workers; industry which is related to skill / crafts, e.g. jewellery / clothing trades or services
- Residential property for affluent residents with city business interests.
- Properties related to the tourist industry such as hotels with need for immediate access to city centre for other entertainment; concentration of certain businesses which benefit from agglomeration, e.g. banks, and other financial institutions.
- High cost of land might exclude other land uses such as parks and low cost housing and smaller retail outlets.

1(b) Assess out of 4 and 3 if no named city given

Depending upon chosen city the answer might include:
- Expansion of the CBD;
- Gentrification of older former high quality residential property;
- slum clearance; rehabilitation of poorer quality properties (e.g. former warehouses turned into high cost flats);
- growth and development of transport network and possible motorway construction;
- older industrial premises replaced with new industrial estates.

Question 2

2(a) Award $\frac{1}{2}$ mark for each feature and $\frac{1}{2}$ mark for each grid reference up to a maximum of 1.

Candidates should be able to identify a range of tourist related features. These might include:
- Museums (3104, 2805, 2806);
- Aquarium (3103);
- railway (3203);
- Royal pavilion (3104);
- Leisure centre (2804);
- Palace Pier (3103).

2(b) Assess out of 6 with a maximum of 4 for area A or Area B. If no reference to site or landscape assess out of 4.

Descriptions might include

Area A –
- 19th century; built on flat land; probably terraced housing; little open space; grid-iron pattern to streets; churches; railway and railway station; Main road (A-class).

Area B –
- Built in 1950s / possibly inter-war; built on steeper land on the edge of Brighton: probably semi-detached housing: curves and cul-de-sacs; street pattern follows contours in places; more open space; B class road nearby.

GLOSSARY OF ASSOCIATED TERMS

Central Business District (CBD): This is the zone which contains the major shops, businesses, offices, restaurants, clubs and other entertainments and is normally located at the center of the settlement at the junction of the main roads.

Commuter settlement: Small settlements on the outskirts of major towns and cities where people live but travel into the main settlement for employment and services.

Commuter: Those who live in commuter settlements

Greenbelts: Areas surrounding cities and towns in which laws control development such as housing and industry in order to protect the countryside.

Inner city: This is the area near the centre which contains basically the CBD, the older manufacturing zone and zone of low cost housing.

Dereliction and decay: Old buildings such as factories and houses which through age, wear and tear are no longer useable and have been abandoned. They cause visual pollution and are often demolished to make way for new developments.

Functions: These are individual activities which settlements perform such as commercial, industrial, administrative, transport, religious, medical, recreational and residential.

Functional zones: These are areas of a settlement where certain functions are dominant, for example industrial zones.

High order functions: These are the most important functions such as department stores, Council offices or Art galleries.

Low order functions: These are less important functions such as small corner shops, post offices and petrol stations.

Overspill population: This refers to people who have moved out of the main city to other smaller towns or new towns.

Pedestrianised zones: These are traffic free areas within the city center where people can shop and walk along streets where traffic is forbidden to enter.

Renewal and regeneration: This refers to the processes by which older areas are demolished and replaced by new buildings often having totally different functions to the original building or area.

Ring roads: Roads built specifically to take traffic away from the city center and to help solve the problem of congestion

Site: This is the actual land upon which a settlement was originally built.

Site factors: These are the factors which influenced people to choose a particular site such as nearness to water supply (river), flat land for building, high land for defence, at a suitable point on a river where a bridge could be built, near raw materials.

Sphere of influence: This is the area from which settlements draws its customers for various functions. Usually the size of the sphere of influence varies in direct response to the size of the settlement.

Suburbs: Housing zones on the outskirts of towns away from the busy central inner city.

Traffic congestion: This is a heavy build up of traffic along major routes and within the city center which causes great problems of cost and pollution for many cities in the UK.

Urban model: This is an idealised view of the internal structure of a settlement and can be used as a basis for comparing settlements.

Environmental Interactions

FOREWORD

ENVIRONMENTAL INTERACTIONS FOREWORD

In the revised Arrangements for Higher Geography, the Applications section of the syllabus and the examination will be renamed 'Environmental Interactions'.
In the external examination you will be required to answer two questions: one Physical Environmental Interaction and one Human Environmental Interaction question.

   The choice of question will have already have been decided for you by your teacher.

In your class studies you will be issued with notes and standard textbooks which will deal with your chosen topics in great detail.

   This section of the revision guide provides a basic set of areas for study within each of the Interactions. These notes are not intended to replace your teaching materials but merely to give you an opportunity to revise the most important points. Consequently, this guide makes only brief reference to example case study material in topics such as Rural land resources, Urban Management and Health and Development.

- It is vital that in answering questions you provide detail from case studies such as a city in a developing country (ELDC).
- Your reference should indicate detailed knowledge of your chosen study area. If you simply make passing reference such as 'an area which I have studied is India' or 'Calcutta', and then proceed to give a very general answer you could lose a significant number of marks.
- The total number of marks for these questions will be 25 marks for each question.
- The marks will be broken down into different topic areas. Unlike questions in the first two sections (the Physical and Human Environment), parts of the Interactions questions may require you to provide long, essay type answers, perhaps worth up to 12 marks.
- In effect you will have to write extended answers dealing with a number of sub-topics and illustrate your answer with appropriate examples.
- Failure to answer any part of the question could result in quite a significant difference in the final grade.
- It is very important that you should take time to read the question carefully. The question will give you a good clue as to how you should break up your answers into sub-sections.
- For example you may be asked to discuss the economic, social and environmental consequences of a particular development such as policies dealing with 'shanty towns'.
- You could take each of these aspects in turn and discuss them whilst making reference to specific examples from countries or cities which you have studied.
- By breaking the question into separate areas, you should have less trouble in writing a long, detailed answer.

- This revision guide provides you with a basic structure for your answer and by adding appropriate detail from your class studies and standard textbook revision throughout the course, you should be able to achieve not only a basic pass, but a highly creditable grade in the final examination.
- If you have time left at the end of your Interactions examination, go back over your answers and ask yourself if you have discussed all of the topics in the question and if you have followed the instructions of the questions to refer to places which you have studied.
- If you find any obvious omissions, go back to that answer and try to complete the answer by adding any appropriate detail which you left out of your original answer.

Even a few minutes spent doing this could result in a grade which is much higher than that which you might otherwise have achieved.

Every minute available to you in the examination should be used productively. There is no point in leaving the examination early and later reading the paper and regretting not providing that little bit extra which could have made all the difference.

The questions tend to be set in a format which would allow you to organise your study of the topics in a manageable manner.

RURAL LAND RESOURCES

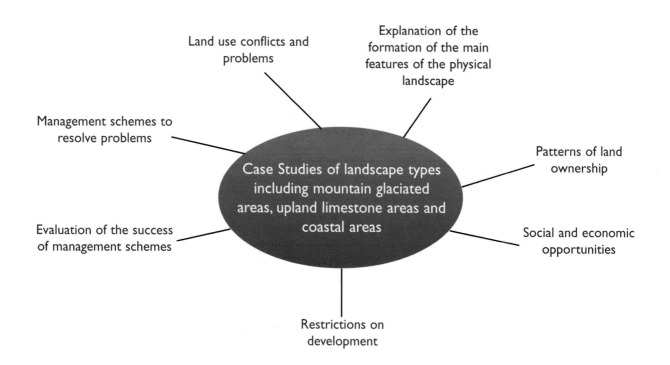

Land use conflicts and problems

Explanation of the formation of the main features of the physical landscape

Management schemes to resolve problems

Patterns of land ownership

Case Studies of landscape types including mountain glaciated areas, upland limestone areas and coastal areas

Evaluation of the success of management schemes

Social and economic opportunities

Restrictions on development

For any named glaciated mountain area in the UK

Key Point 1

You should be able to describe and explain the formation of a range of glaciated features – with the aid of annotated diagrams

The features that you should know include
Feaures of erosion
U-shaped valleys, hanging valleys, pyramidal peaks, corries, corrie lakes (tarns), arêtes, truncated spurs, ribbon lakes, misfit streams, alluvial fans.
Features of glacial deposition
moraines, eskers, drumlins, crag and tail, outwash plains. The description and explanation of their formation are discussed in detail within the Lithosphere section of physical environments (see pages 54–58).

Key Point 2

You should know the factors which limit human activity and explain why this landscape attracts tourists but restricts other economic activities

Farming is restricted to mainly hill sheep farming due to the difficulty of the terrain and the poor quality of soils. Settlement is also restricted to valley areas where it is possible to build on flatter ground. The same is true of communication routes. A lack of raw materials due to the geology of the area has limited industrial development to, e.g. quarrying.

Tourists are attracted to the splendid scenery of these areas for purposes such as hillwalking, mountaineering and skiing. The Cairngorms in northern Scotland is a good example of an area that possesses all of the scenic qualities to attract large numbers of tourists throughout the year. Although many upland glaciated areas have their human activities restricted due to their remoteness and inaccessibility, it is often this factor which attracts tourists to the area for the peace and quiet of the environment.

For any named upland limestone area in the UK

Key Point 3

You should be able to using annotated diagrams describe and explain relief and drainage (both surface and underground) and explain the restrictions on economic development of this landscape

Features which you should *recognise*, *describe* and *explain* include, intermittant drainage, limestone pavements, clints and grykes, potholes, underground caverns, stalagmites and stalactites, underground lakes, scarp slopes and scree. Refer to the Lithosphere chapter (see pages 58–59) for more details on the description and formation of these features.

Key Point 4

For a named coastal area you should be able to describe and explain the formation of features such as headlands, bays, stacks, caves, arches, spits, tombolos and longshore drift

Refer to the Lithosphere section (see pages 60–62) for description and explanation of these features.

Key Point 5

For an upland area or coastal area you have studied, you should be able to explain the opportunities for social and economic development, the effect of visitors on the local populace and the restrictions on development. You should provide detailed discussion on environmental conflicts in the area and how they are resolved

You can refer to any of the national parks in England and Wales or those in Scotland. Opportunities for development include **property, industrial, recreational, tourism** and **commercial** development. Development will be restricted to those which meet the standards of national park legislation.

Figure 1·1 – National Parks and main centres of population

Developments such as industry or housing must not detract from the landscape in terms of for example visual pollution, e.g. quarries scarring the landscape or housing which is not in character with existing housing styles.

Developments such as these may bring **advantages** such as:
- Employment opportunity in, e.g. hotels, shops, building trades and the tourist industry in general.
- More money is put into the local economy of villages and towns through tourists.
- Improvements in the local infrastructure, e.g. road and railway facilities being improved. Facilities for local population being improved, e.g. new libraries, clinics, leisure facilities.

Disadvantages resulting from new developments include:
- Increased demand for new property, particularly holiday accommodation.
- Purchase of local housing for second homes thus depriving local populace of housing opportunity or increased prices in property.
- Increased traffic congestion and danger on local roads due to increase in visitors.
- Increases in various forms of pollution through litter, traffic, vandalism and possible increases in land erosion, e.g. footpaths.

- Danger to farmland and forested areas from, e.g. disregard for safety of livestock (gates left open, animals frightend by dogs) and fires.
- Pollution of water areas, e.g. lakes from watersport activites, e.g. motorboats.

Solutions included:
- Environmental conflicts resolved by national park authorities and other conservation agencies strictly enforcing rules and legislation on anyone causing deliberate damage. Limitations imposed on certain activities, e.g. watersports can reduce environmental damage.
- Education centres have been set up to educate visitors on proper use of facilities and areas within national parks whilst observing the need to respect the natural environment.
- The difficulty lies in trying to strike the balance between encouraging visitors and taking measures to limit damaging effects.
- The impact of increased public access to parks is therefore continually and carefully monitored to maintain the sustainability of national parks.

Key Point 6

You should be able to explain why land ownership patterns can make the management of National Parks difficult and argue the case for and against national parks in Scotland

There is a wide variety of land owners within national parks including, farmers, golf courses, local industry, e.g. quarries, national government, e.g. main roads / motorways, householders, water board and owners of sites of historical and cultural importance, Ministry of Defence, Forestry Commision and National Trust. Many of these land users can be in conflict with each other and with the aims of the national park authorities since they may wish to develop the land in different ways.

Loch Lomond National Park was designated in 1997. The area was granted national park status in 2000 and Scotland's second national park, the Cairngorms, was designated in 2003.

Arguments in favour of park status for Loch Lomond included:
- The need to protect the physical environment of the area including the actual loch from any developments which would detract from or spoil the landscape.
- The area has been subjected to constant demand for development from a wide variety of activities including, water board, tourism, recreational, marina developments, communications, housing, industrial and agricultural.
- The need to provide good access and facilities for public open air enjoyment and maintain established farmland.

RURAL LAND DEGRADATION

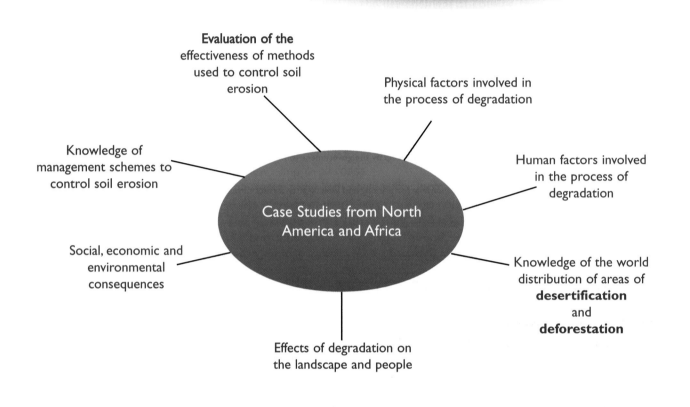

Evaluation of the effectiveness of methods used to control soil erosion

Physical factors involved in the process of degradation

Knowledge of management schemes to control soil erosion

Human factors involved in the process of degradation

Case Studies from North America and Africa

Social, economic and environmental consequences

Knowledge of the world distribution of areas of **desertification** and **deforestation**

Effects of degradation on the landscape and people

Key Point 1
Referring to a detailed case study in North America and either Africa north of the equator or the Amazon basin, you should be able to describe the factors which led to severe land degradation

For the Dust Bowl in the USA

Physical factors include:
- The area is located far from sea thus reducing rainfall.
- The Rocky mountains to the west produced a rainshadow effect from eastward flowing air which also reduced rainfall.
- Moist air generally flows north from the Gulf of Mexico during the summer.
- If this veers to the north-east the Great Plains would lose rainfall.

Human factors include:
- Monoculture, especially growing wheat or cotton depleted the soil of moisture and nutrients.
- Soils were ploughed deeply adding to their already fragile state.
- Ploughing of marginal land during wet years which left them fragile during dry years. Overcropping of small farms during periods when prices were low.
- Overgrazing of land on the western margin of plains.

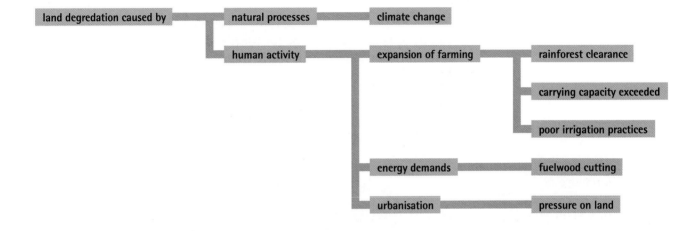

Figure 2·1 – Processes in land degradation

For the Tennessee Valley, USA

Physical factors include:
*   The presence of many steep slopes throughout the area.
*   Rainfall occuring mainly as heavy storms rather than a more regular pattern.

Human factors include:
*   Deforestation of the area leaving the soils exposed to erosion.
*   Natural vegetation which protected the soil removed due to mining and farming increasing soil erosion.
*   Steep slopes ploughed up and down the slopes and overcropping which weakened the soil further.
*   Use of inappropriate farming techniques, e.g. monoculture.

Key Point 2
You should be able to explain the main processes of wind erosion

*   If topsoil is dry and loosened or exposed by agriculture, it may be blown away by strong winds. If there is no surface protection from trees or vegetation the erosive effect of the wind increases.
*   If most of the top soil is blown away the land becomes stripped of nutrients and is unable to sustain crop growth.
*   In the 1930s millions of hectares of farmland was lost in the worst example of wind erosion in the area known as the Dust Bowl of the mid-western states of the USA.
*   Fine particles to which organanic material is attached is removed and soil dust carried by wind in suspension can be deposited burying fields and killing growing plants.

Key Point 3

You be able to describe the location and distribution of areas of desertification shown on a world map

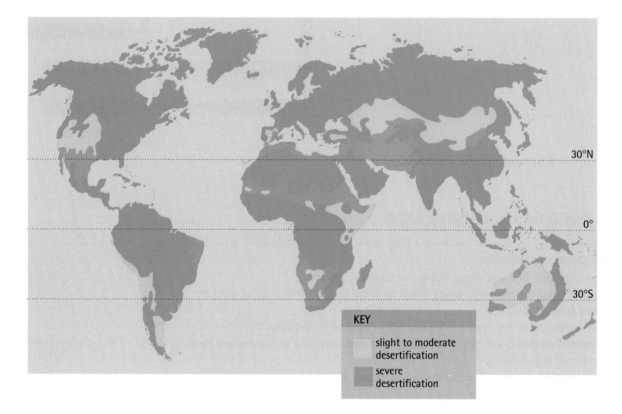

KEY

slight to moderate desertification

severe desertification

Figure 2·2 – Pattern of world desertification

- Refer to the general location of areas where desertification is taking place, e.g. the Sahel
- Refer to areas where the process is most severe
- Refer to specific locations if possible within different continents, e.g. north Africa; south west Africa – Namibia.

Key Point 4

You should be able to describe rainfall patterns shown on given maps and diagrams and explain how rainfall variability can contribute to soil erosion and land degradation

- Describe the patterns in terms of areas of high / low (deficit) rainfall;
- Note the high and low seasons;
- Note that extended periods of low rainfall can cause vegetation to die;
- Dead vegetation may be removed by action of wind or water thus removing protection of surface cover;

- Exposed soil may be eroded by wind or flash floods;
- The remaining soils loses fertility and nutrients and are unable to sustain growth due to lack of water;
- The land and soil becomes degraded.

Key Point 5

You should be able to describe and explain how deforestation and certain farming practices (e.g. monoculture can lead to soil erosion)

- Deforestation removes tree cover and exposes underlying soil and vegetation to effects of sun The sun dries out soil causing leaching and formation of lateritic surface.
- Overcultivation exhausts soil of nutrients;
- Growing the same crop continuously exhausts the soil of its fertility;
- Removal of trees for firewood removes protection and exposes soil to effects of wind erosion;
- Overgrazing removes protective surface vegetation;
- If farmers fail to replenish nutrients with fertilisers soil becomes thin and unable to sustain growth.

Key Point 6

You should know the main effects of vegetation removal on land and people

Effects include:
- An inability of farmers to graze animals
- Soils which are exposed to elements and are eroded and therefore unable to sustain crop growth
- Famine which may occur due to low crop yields
- People may migrate to other areas
- Traditional farming, e.g. pastoral nomadism may disappear
- Removal of vegetation may impact on local or global climates, leading to the greenhouse efffect
- Removal of vegetation can increase ground water run-off rates and possibly lead to flooding.

Key Point 7

You should be able to describe the impact of rural land degradation on people and land and know the social, economic and environmental consequences

For North America

Impact on people and social / economic consequences:

- Land and crops destroyed
- Farmers abandoned land and migrated to other areas to find work, e.g. from Oklahoma to California
- Those who remained experienced great poverty.

Impact on land and environmental consequences:

- Lack of cover to protect land and therefore soil blew away
- Desertification of countryside and dust storms
- Soil is exhausted of nutrients and incapable of sustaining crop growth.

For the Amazon Basin

Impact on people and social / economic consequences:

- Destruction of way of life for local people and clashes between locals and incomers. Destruction of formerly sustainable activities such as rubber tappers
- A reduction of fallow periods causing reduced yields leading to food shortages
- The impact of large business interests acting in conflict with local interests
- The migration of local people away from traditional habitats; increased poverty and social deprivation.

Impact on land and environmental consequences:

- Impact of deforestation on nutrient cycle which causes leaching and laterisation of soils exposed to the elements
- There is increased run off of ground water and flooding
- There is a loss of wildlife habitats
- There are wider effects on global climates through the greenhouse effect.

For Africa north of equator

Impact on people and social / economic consequences:

- Crop failures and consequently malnutrition leading to major famines, e.g. Ethiopia/Sudan There are mass migrations often to refugee camps or shanty towns on edge of cities
- There is often a collapse of traditional activities, e.g. nomadism due to overgrazing and lack of water
- There is increased pressure on land due to nomads settling in villages
- This results in increased tensions between nomads and traditional farmers
- There may be widespread desperate poverty and deprivation
- This results in increased mortality rates especially infant mortality rates.

Impact on land and environmental consequences:

- There is a breakdown of soil structure
- This causes an advance of the Sahara desert resulting in the process of desertification
- There is wind erosion of dried out soils
- There is also erosion from rains when they eventually arrive
- Water tables are also lowered
- There may be an impact on local climate due to lack of moisture recycling.

Key Point 8

You should be able to describe various methods of soil conservation and how these methods help reduce land degradation adding suitable comment on their effectiveness

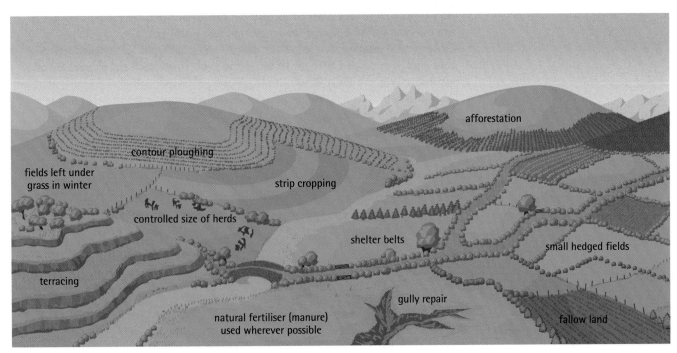

Figure 2·3 – Soil conservation measures

For Africa north of the equator solutions may include:

- Building dams, e.g. parts of Kenya
- Planting trees as windbreaks
- Stabilising dunes with grass, e.g. parts of Mali
- Terracing slopes to prevent erosion
- Improved irrigation. Even small scale schemes are very effective in increasing soil depth and crop yields.
- Controlled grazing and fencing are also very effective in preventing top vegetation being removed thus exposing soil to wind erosion.

For Amazon Basin measures might include:

- Reafforestation with mixed trees
- The use of crop rotation by farmers
- The purchase of forest areas by conservation groups
- Returning forests to native peoples.
- Several schemes are very effective but outside interests in mining, ranching etc., often take precedence over conservation measures.
- Flooding due to deforestion can remove soil and mining causes increased pollution.
- There have been attempts to control this through government legislation but the impact has been limited to economic demands for development.

For North America measures include:
- Contour ploughing and crop rotation
- Extensive use of fertilisers
- Widespread access to irigation schemes
- Leaving fields fallow
- Government subsidies for farmers
- Improved mechanisation.
- All of these measures have been very successful but often very expensive, e.g. use of chemical fertilisers; genetically modified (GM) crops.
- Government intervention, e.g. river management schemes for irrigation and subsidies have helped farmers to avoid the problems which led to severe soil erosion in, e.g. the Dust Bowl.
- Soil protection is a major part of agricultural development and regarded as a having significant priority.

GLOSSARY OF ASSOCIATED TERMS

Cattle ranching: Rearing of large herds of cattle on areas of cleared forests to provide beef to be sold for export.

Deforestation: Removal of trees usually on a large scale

Degradation: The process of reducing land which was formely productive into unproductive land.

Desertification: Process of turning land which was formerly productive into desert

Drought: Prolonged periods without rainfall which may last from several months to several years.

Food chain: A system whereby various forms of life provide food for each other starting at one point and finishing at another, e.g. from small fish to larger and eventually to humans.

Global warming: The heating up of the earth's atmosphere by the sun's rays due to the effects of atmospheric pollution

Greenhouse effect: This is a natural effect which is caused by a number of gases (carbon dioxide, methane, nitrous oxide, chlorofluorocarbons and ozone) present in the upper atmosphere. These gases help to trap heat energy in the earth's atmosphere by absorbing and reflecting long-wave solar radiation. Increases in these greenhouse gases (due to the effects of industrialisation) may well be a contributing factor to global climate change.

Greenpeace: An international organisation which organises protests against the causes of world pollution and other elements which destroy the natural environment

Insecticides: Chemicals used by farmers to kill insects which feed on crops.

Irrigation: An artificial way of providing water for farming from sources such as rivers, wells, canals, field sprays.

Logging: A commercial business which cuts down trees to provide timber for sale for different purposes.

Overcropping: Growing crops continually to the extent that the soil becomes exhausted of nutrients, becomes infertile and unable to sustain further growth.

Overgrazing: Allowing animals to overeat grass to the extent that the underlying soil is exposed and cannot sustain further growth.

Marginal land: Land which is on the outer limit of sustainable growth and development where crop growth is only just possible.

Nomadism: The system whereby people migrate with animals throughout the year to find new areas for grazing livestock also known as 'Pastoral Nomadism'.

Pollutants: Material which is released into the environment which ultimately causes damage to the physical landscape and atmosphere.

Power stations: Complexes which are built to provide electricity from various sources such as nuclear energy, fossil fuels and water.

Reafforestation: This is the process of replanting trees in former forested areas.

Shelter belt: A line of trees planted to provide shelter from the wind for fields by interrupting the flow of wind.

Soil conservation: Attempts to protect soil from damage using methods such as fertilisers, irrigation, shelter belts and ploughing along contours and using terraces to conserve soil.

Soil erosion: The process by which the topsoil is removed leaving the land infertile.

Tundra: An area of cold, desert located only in the northern hemisphere. It lies between the northern limits of tree growth and the areas of permanent snow and ice.

Windbreaks: Trees which interrupt the flow of wind so as to protect fields and their crops.

RIVER BASIN MANAGEMENT

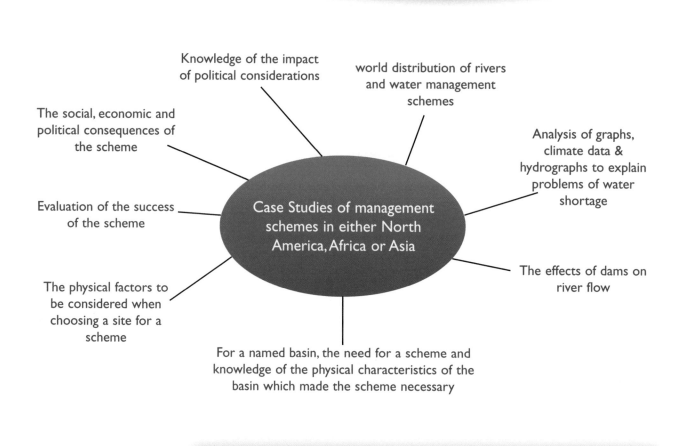

Knowledge of the impact of political considerations

world distribution of rivers and water management schemes

The social, economic and political consequences of the scheme

Analysis of graphs, climate data & hydrographs to explain problems of water shortage

Evaluation of the success of the scheme

Case Studies of management schemes in either North America, Africa or Asia

The effects of dams on river flow

The physical factors to be considered when choosing a site for a scheme

For a named basin, the need for a scheme and knowledge of the physical characteristics of the basin which made the scheme necessary

Key Point 1

Referring to either North America, Africa or Asia, you should be able to describe and explain the general distributions of river basins and water control projects

See Figure 3·1
- Depending on the area chosen, you may refer to:
- General patterns of distribution and the number of rivers
- Directions of flow and explanation may refer to mountain ranges as major sources of rivers, e.g. Ethiopian Highlands, due to their greater rainfall
- Climate patterns throughout the area
- Places where river basins meet sea/oceans.

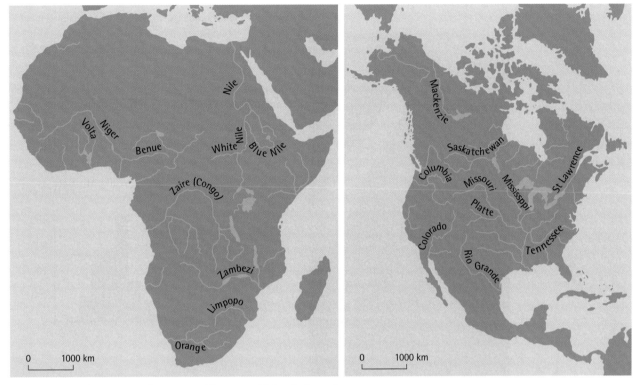

Figure 3·1 – Major river basins in Africa and North America

Key Point 2

Using a range of maps, climate graphs, hydrographs etc., for any river basin in North America or Africa you should be able to explain why there is a water supply problem and why a water storage scheme is essential. You should also be able to describe ways in which the river's flow has changed since the building of dams and be able to outline the advantages and disadvantages of water storage in areas of permeable and impermeable rock

For the figures given for the Nile Valley (see Figure 3·2):
- You should note the wide seasonal fluctuations in discharge levels
- The steady flow of 100-500 million cumecs between November and May, rising to 200 million cumecs in June
- A rapid rise in July to a peak discharge of 900 million cumecs in late August / early September, with an equally sharp decline in October.

Explanation
- The July – September surge is due to pronounced seasonal regime of Blue Nile's catchment area in the Ethiopian Highlands (see climate graph for Bahr Dar).
- The more regular flow of the White Nile with its source in East Africa (Lake Victoria) helps compensate for the dry season in Ethiopia.
- This maintains water levels at a steady level for the remainder of the year.

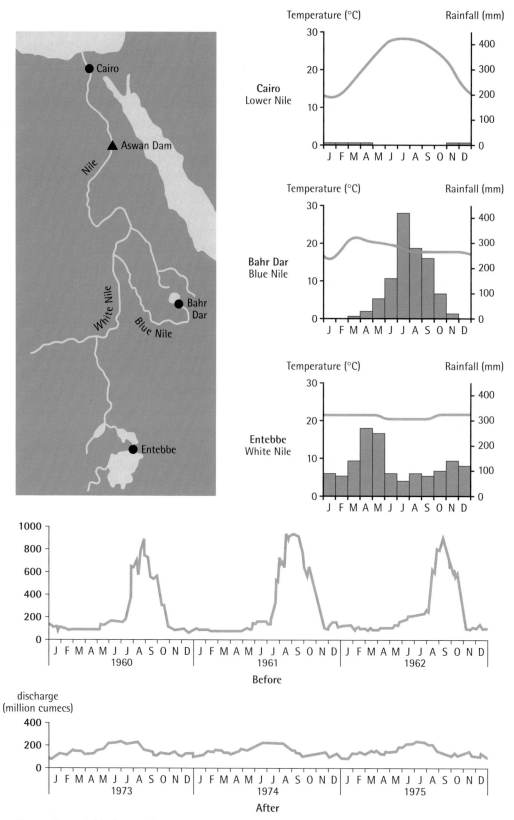

Figure 3·2 – Nile basin data

Change
- The flow of the river has been even and regular since the Aswan dam was built.
- Extremes giving rise to annual floods no longer occur. Despite slight fluctuations, maximum discharge rarely exceeds 250 million cumecs.
- The dam clearly controls river flow.

Referring to a named river basin (e.g. River Nile or Colorado) which you have studied:

Key Point 3

You should know why there was a need for river basin management referring to factors such as climate, landforms, environmental problems

Depending on basin chosen, your answer may refer to:
- The rainfall pattern especially periods of low rainfall
- Any seasonal droughts
- Any navigation problems due to physical features of river valley
- The need for water transfer to areas of deficit
- The irrigation potential and flood control during high rain season
- Any HEP potential and the suitability of underlying geology (impermeable rock) for water storage schemes and dam construction.

Key Point 4

You should know the physical and human factors which influence the choice of site for dams and reservoirs

Answers should refer to:
- The need for solid foundations for a dam
- The need for a narrow cross-section to reduce dam length
- A large deep valley to flood behind the dam
- A sufficient water flow from catchment area
- Local evaporation rates
- The permeability of underlying rock.
- The amount of farmland which would be flooded
- The number of settlements which would be flooded
- Local population distribution
- The distance from urban or farming areas for HEP or irrigation.

Key Point 5

You should know how the scheme impacts on the hydrological cycle of the basin

You should refer to:
- Increased evaporation from surface area of massive reservoirs
- The impact on local climate
- There is less water flowing below dams
- Often rivers are diverted
- Water table levels are changing
- infiltration rates are affected by water held in reservoirs or irrigation channels.

Key Point 6

You should be able to describe and explain the social, economic and environmental effects of the water control project on the basin and be able to assess the success of the scheme in terms of its social, political and evironmental impact

Your answer will depend on river project chosen, but may refer to the following:

Social Benefits
- Greater population helped by increased food supply
- There is less disease and poor health due to better water supply and more food becoming available
- There may be more recreational opportunities
- There is more widespread availability of electricity

Social adverse consequences
There will be forced removal of people from valley sites and increased incidence of water-borne diseases, e.g. Bilharzia, schistosomiasis, river blindness.

Economic benefits
- Improved yields in farming
- HEP (hydro-electric power) which is helping to create industrial development
- More water for industry
- Improved navigation channels

Economic adverse consequences
- It could involve a huge expenditure on the new scheme
- A dependence on foreign finance resulting in increased debt
- More money being needed for fertilisers / compensation etc.

Environmental benefits
- There is an increase in fresh water supply
- There are improvements in sanitation and health
- There are also improvements in scenic value
- There is the bonus of flood control

Environmental adverse effects
- Water pollution and industrial pollution increases
- There is an increase in silting of reservoirs
- There is also increased salinity rates further downstream
- There may be possible flooding of historical sites

Key Point 7

You should also know the political problems which may have resulted from management project(s) and how political considerations might hinder the project(s)

- Political problems depend on chosen river basin but might include:
- Water control or dependence on neighbours upstream
- Complex legislation over appropriate water sharing by different states or counties
- Reduced flow and increased salinity in some areas
- Shared costs between states or different authorities or problems over allocation of costs Increase pollution across borders resulting in problems of allocating appropriate costs of cleaning the river.

GLOSSARY OF ASSOCIATED TERMS

Drainage: This is the term used to describe all surface water in a river system and should not be confused with underground pipes used to drain water from bog or marshland.

Environmental consequences: This refers to the net effects on the physical and human environments of changes to river basins through physical or human changes.

Infiltration: The process by which water from precipitatin seeps into the soil and sub soil.

River basin: This is the water catchment area of a river and includes the main river and its tributaries.

Salinity: This is the salt content in surface water such as rivers, streams and lakes.

Seasonal fluctuation: This happens when the normal climatic pattern is interrupted for example when there is a change to rainfall distribution which could result in drought.

Silting: This is the amount of sand and other material carried in solution in rivers and when deposited can reduce river flow.

Tributary: This is a smaller river or stream which runs into a larger river.

Water control project: This is the name given to efforts to manage various aspects of a river basin such as river flow, reservoirs, silting, navigation and river discharge; for example through the use of dams, canals, acquducts and diversion schemes.

Key Point 2

You should be able to suggest reasons for increasing traffic congestion

Traffic congestion has increased in both developed and developing world cities due to:

*   Increased volume of motor vehicles on roads linked to commuter traffic from rural / urban fringe areas surrounding developed world cities
*   Poor quality roads within inner city areas unable to cope with volume of traffic
*   Increasing population within developing world cities moving into inner city areas for employment.
*   Lack of adequate public transport services in most cities.
*   Lack of investment in the infrastructure within developing countries.

Key Point 3

You should be able to describe and explain the distribution of cities in a given developed or developing country

Figure 4·2 – Distribution of cities in USA

Depending on the country or countries you have studied you could include a range of factors.

For USA factors include:

- Favourable locations including coastal location such as the Florida and Californian coast and the North Eastern Seaboard with Boston, New York and Washington (Bosnywash).
- Natural routeways through major valleys or along coastal plains.
- Access to raw materials such as iron ore, coal, oil and precious minerals.
- Lakeside locations and favourable climates such as Lake Michigan.
- Avoiding certain areas include mountain areas such as the Rockies/Appalachians; desert areas, e.g. Arizona; areas of extensive farming.

For Brazil factors include:

- Most of Brazil's cities are located on the coast, e.g. Rio de Janeiro, Sao Paulo and Recife due to advantages such as availability of flat land, accessibility, coastal location having advantages for development of port / fishing industries.
- Few large settlements are found inland due to the presence of the rainforest.
- The most notable exception is the capital Brasilia which was purposely built inland to encourage the development of the forested areas.

Key Point 4

You should be able to describe and explain variations in land use values within cities

Variations include:

- Highest land values being closest to city centre, i.e. CBD and Industrial zone due to factors such as accessibility, ability to pay highest rents and rates.
- Inner city housing areas closest to industry tend to have low cost housing but because housing in very high density, land value tends to be higher in terms of rent returns.
- Medium and Higher cost housing is found further away from city centre where the environment suffers less from traffic congestion and pollution.
- Although property values are higher in these areas, land values are lower due to much lower density of housing.
- Peripheral areas attract land uses such as superstores, industrial estates and recreational activities due to relatively lower land values.

Key Point 5

You should be able to determine the accuracy of statements relating to urban patterns as shown in a variety of maps and diagrams

- Diagrams and maps may contain data such as property values, density, land use, employment statistics etc. which require you to evaluate.
- Evaluations often depend on your understanding of city models of developed and developing world cities.
- Use data given in the question to support your arguments.

Key Point 6

For a named city in the Developed world you should be able to describe and explain the human and physical factors responsible for its growth

For New York factors include

Human factors:

- The historical development with early settlers arriving in this area from European countries.
- Nodal position for trade with Europe.
- Development of major industries, e.g. textiles, port industries.
- Being an immigration point for people arriving from European countries and settling in the city during the 19th and 20th centuries.

Physical factors:

- A deep water location for large ships.
- The city having a commanding strategic position at seaward end of Hudson Mohawk gap. The city having been built on islands – Manhattan.

Key Point 7

With reference to a named city you have studied in the developed world, you should be able to describe and explain the distribution of shopping centres

You might refer to Glasgow and mention factors such as:

- In Glasgow the CBD lies on the north bank of the River Clyde stretching two kilometres east / west and approximately one kilometre north.
- There are several secondary shopping centres throughout the city with a wide range of shops from convenience strores to supermarkets, clothes shops and furniture / electrical goods in areas such as Partick, Shawlands, Maryhill.
- Other areas within the city are served by neighbourhood shopping centres with a more limited range of shops, primarily convenience shops such as chemists, newsagents and foodstores such as Spar.
- This pattern is basically explained by factors such as the type of demand (less important shops require a smaller number of customers, more important shops have customers willing to travel greater distances, e.g. to the CBD which contains the largest shops).
- Cost of land affects location with only the larger outlets able to afford the highest costs at city centre locations.

Key Point 8

Describe the ways in which problems such as industrial decline, poor housing and pollution have been tackled and comment on the effectiveness of the solution

Industrial decline:
*   In the years since the end of the second world war, many of Britain's older, traditional industries have gone into economic decline including shipbuilding, iron and steel, textiles and heavy engineering.
*   Many of the large industrial areas of the cities have become abandoned. Factories have been demolished for safety reasons but the former sites have been left as 'gap sites'.
*   In many cases these gap sites have been bought by property developers who have been able to build and sell a variety of development schemes including new housing, shopping and recreational buildings such as sports centres.
*   Land near the city centre offers attractive sites for the right development. Other industrial sites have been replaced by industrial estates built in areas where they might not be expected to be found, that is in the inner city areas.
*   Cities which had port and shipbuilding industries often have large areas of dockland which is no longer in use.
*   In Glasgow, Liverpool and London these dockland areas have undergone major changes and now contain a wide variety of new land uses such as new housing, conference centres and hotels and a variety of shopping, tourist and other service functions.
*   These have been very successful and have changed the environments of these former industrial areas completely.
*   Brownfield sites of former manufacturing industry have been developed as new industrial / trading estates and science parks.

Poor housing:
*   Many parts of cities have buildings which through age and lack of care have fallen into disrepair.
*   These buildings may be industrial buildings, housing, office blocks or even shopping areas. Their visual appearance may be unsightly and more importantly they may be unsafe for use or habitation.
*   If they are no longer in use they may become decayed. Often these buildings are left for many years before action is taken.
*   Common sites for them include being near railway lines, canals, inner city housing areas, along the banks of rivers and perhaps at the edges of the central business area.
*   The problem is often lack of money for demolition and redevelopment.
*   However, many cities have made great efforts to remove these buildings and replace them with newer buildings.
*   New buildings include office blocks, new housing, recreational centres and occasional under cover shopping centres.
*   These changes have often been achieved through the financial assistance of government grants and even European Union grants.

Pollution:

- Pollution includes river pollution from industries discharging waste, urban blight caused by derelict buildings, litter, vandalism, air pollution from industries and traffic.
- Pollution from industries, motor vehicles or neglect can accumulate to such an extent that it can not only destroy the appearance of some parts of cities, the pollutants may be a health hazard.
- Measures which have been taken to tackle these problems include the introduction of smokeless zones, building of high chimneys, banning of industries which are the source of obnoxious smells or pollutants.
- City councils employ environmental health departments to implement laws and regulations to monitor and control pollution. Although this is costly, the benefits are obvious to the residents of cities.
- All of these problems have been successfully tackled in Glasgow due to measures such as clean up programmes on the River Clyde and more recently the Forth and Clyde canal, ring roads and pedestrianisation of areas within the CBD diverting traffic from the city centre.
- Many have improved facilities to the extent that they have won awards such as British city of Architecture and Culture awards.

Key Point 9

You should be able to explain the factors causing traffic congestion and assess efforts to reduce traffic congestion

Problems:

- Problems of traffic congestion are due to factors such as the quality of roads leading into city centre, huge volume of commuter traffic at peak times, lack of or cost of public transport services, cars parking on main roads and lack of parking facilities within city centre.
- Traffic is one of the most difficult problems which cities have had to deal with in recent years.
- The volume of traffic has increased tremendously with huge amounts of private and commercial vehicles entering and leaving city areas through the day.
- The problem is at its greatest during the morning and evening rush hours. However weekend traffic is often just as bad.
- This has led to problems of congestion, accidents, damage to roads, high costs of road maintenance and disruption to the life and work of the city.

Measures taken:

- Changes to road systems such as ring roads; one-way systems; use of 'bus only' lanes; contra-flow systems; widening of roads; building by-passes; and, in the case of Glasgow, having a motorway going through the city centre to speed up the flow of traffic.
- Parking restrictions are also used to prevent parked cars blocking main routes. These are enforced by police and traffic wardens.
- Provision of alternative means of transport to encourage drivers to leave their cars outside the city (such as park and ride schemes, cheap public transport, underground systems, road / rail links) have all been tried.

- There are suggestions that drivers commuting to the city should be charged additional taxes on their cars in the form of tolls and charges for private parking places.
- Preventing people from coming into the city however can create problems especially for shopkeepers and other business which rely on customers for their existence.
- Offering alternatives such as out of town shopping centres may help to solve traffic problems but it can lead to the decline of the Central Business District from which a large proportion of local government finance is obtained.
- Authorities have to balance their solutions very carefully.
- Other solutions include use of park and ride schemes, bus / taxi lanes, one-way systems, by-passes, ring roads, improved public transport services, parking restrictions, pedestrian zones. Despite these efforts, both Glasgow and London experience tremendous difficulties with traffic every day of the week including weekends.
- National government policies recognise this and possible legislation may include tolls on cars entering the city, increased fuel prices and upgrade of railways and other public transport services.

Key Point 10
Describe and explain problems related to the CBD and inner city areas and their solutions

Problems include:
- Closure of shops due to increased competion from out of town shopping centres.
- Declining custom due to movement of population to areas outwith the city, e.g. New Towns.
- Increased rental and rates of properties in the CBD.
- Accessibility problems especially for car owners for example expensive parking fees.
- Inner city areas suffer from traffic congestion, narrow streets, poor quality housing, pollution and declining industrial areas with derelict sites causing urban blight.
- In Glasgow, solutions include housing programmes sponsored by city councils both inner city and outer city schemes such as Castlemilk, Drumchapel, the Great East Area Redevelopment (GEAR) scheme and New Gorbals private housing project.
- Within the CBD in Glasgow several under cover shopping centres have been built including Princess Sqare, St. Enoch's centre and the Buchanan centre.

Solutions include:
- To encourage population back to the city (such as those who left to settle in commuter villages or new towns) several buildings such as warehouses and the former General Post Offices have been converted into modern flats.
- By-passes, one-way systems, park and ride schemes, demolition of abandoned industrial sites, rehabilitation of older housing areas have been introduced to improve the inner city areas.
- All of these efforts have met with considerable success.

Key Point 11

You should be able to suggest why many people have moved outwards from the city and then discuss land use conflicts which have arisen as a consequence of this movement

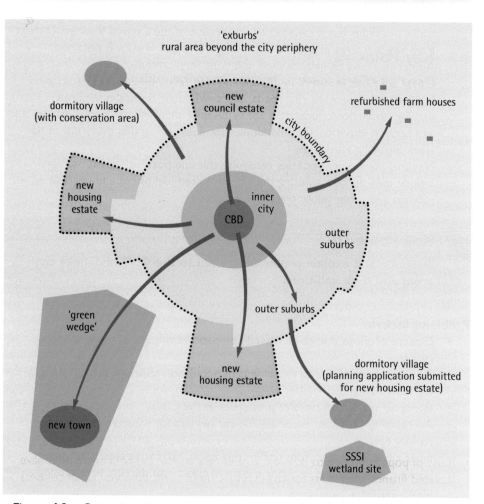

'exburbs'
rural area beyond the city periphery

dormitory village
(with conservation area)

new
council estate

refurbished farm houses

city boundary

new
housing
estate

inner
city

CBD

outer
suburbs

'green
wedge'

outer suburbs

new town

new
housing estate

dormitory village
(planning application submitted
for new housing estate)

SSSI
wetland site

Figure 4·3 – Out-migration patterns around a developed world city

- The population of many cities has decreased as many people left to live in various settlements outside the main city.
- Large numbers of people were prepared to pay the cost of increased travel in terms of time and money to live in what they considered a better environment. Basically, small rural villages were colonised and have become commuter settlements.
- The populations of these former rural villages have often grown enormously. The services provided for their population often bear no relation to their population size. Residents commute to work and purchase most of what they need outwith the villages.
- In other cases, large numbers of people from cities were offered the chance to move to New Towns with the promise of employment as well as housing.

- Many New Towns were built throughout Britain with a wide variety of services, entertainment, schools, and most importantly a wide selection of houses.
- These new towns were very popular. for example East Kilbride is the largest and most successful of Scotland's new towns with a population of about 75,000.
- The result of these movements was that population of cities and the income from this population decreased alarmingly.
- Cities need people to support their services.

Key Point 12

Describe efforts made to reverse or contain this outward movement

- Many cities have tried to attract population back by investing in new a better housing, shopping areas and by trying to attract new industry.
- This is an on going struggle but a number of large cities including Birmingham, Glasgow and Edinburgh have been successful.
- A great deal of money has been invested in upgrading older properties close to the city centres of many cities and making them attractive housing areas. The idea is to attract more and more people from the commuter settlements into the city. This is done by proving that these people can benefit from living in a reasonably pleasant environment without having to pay large sums of money on transport costs and having to endure long difficult journeys to work each day.
- The process of re-populating these inner city areas has been termed 'gentrification'.

Key Point 13

Describe problems caused by de-centralisation of population and the efforts to resolve them

- Loss of population due to development of new towns and commuter belts have created financial problems for city councils, traffic problems and loss of business for city centre shopping areas.
- On the rural-urban fringe, developments such as housing and new industrial estates have led to urban sprawl and loss of rural land.
- This has caused conflict between traditional rural activities such as farming and new developments.
- Greenbelt legislation introduced in the 1950s was an attempt to curb development in rural fringe areas and has been quite successful.
- Limitations on the number and type of buildings have kept the rural environment protected from the worst excesses of city developers.

Key Point 14

Outline the land use conflicts in the rural urban fringe area and explain how Greenbelt policy has helped to resolve them

- Property speculation and compulsory purchase of land by developers has led to a decline in the quality of the rural-urban fringe around many cities.
- This has resulted in loss of farmland and recreational land. As the commuter belt expanded there was ever increasing demand for new houses. This in turn led to increase in traffic on rural roads throughout weeekdays.
- Greenbelt strategies involved planning restrictions and restrictions on developments such as housing, industry, landfill sites and recreational centres.
- Smaller towns and villages have been identified for growth. In central Scotland new towns and overspill areas such as East Kilbride were used as growth centres to limit further development within the rural urban fringe.
- However, small rural villages remained popular with people wishing to leave the city and were still a target for building developers.
- The needs of industry and opportunity for offering employment has had to be balanced with the desire to protect the rural urban fringe.
- Due to the above factors protection efforts, despite greenbelt legislation, have not always been successful.

For a city you have studied in the developing world:

Key Point 15

Compare and contrast land use patterns in a given city in the developing world with that shown in a model of urban structure

- Refer to Figure 4·4, which shows a model of a developing world city.
- Depending on the city which you have studied make a series of statements which compare and contrast the main features of the city with the model.
- Your statement might refer to the location of the CBD and the location of the other main land use zones, i.e. housing, industry, old colonial areas, squatter areas and shanty town areas.
- Differences may be due to site features such as the presence of a river, coastal location, new improvements (e.g. new housing areas such as in Sao Paulo).
- You must be able to refer to specific locations within your chosen city so as to show detailed knowledge rather than general knowledge.
- If you do not show detailed knowledge of a specific location you will forfeit marks.

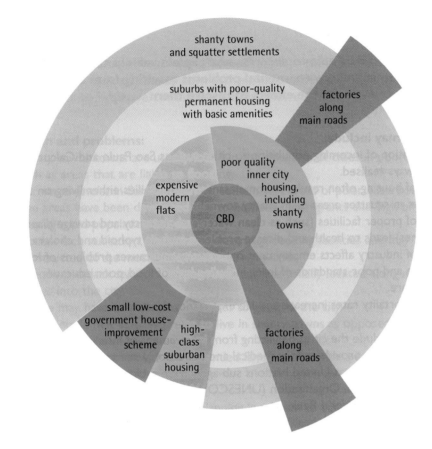

shanty towns
and squatter settlements

suburbs with poor-quality
permanent housing
with basic amenities

factories
along
main roads

poor quality
inner city
housing,
including
shanty
towns

expensive
modern
flats

CBD

small low-cost
government house-
improvement
scheme

high-
class
suburban
housing

factories
along
main roads

Figure 4·4 – Model of a developing world city

Key Point 16

You should be able to describe and explain the factors involved in its site and growth including growth factors such as urban pull and rural push

Sao Paulo can be used as a good example.

Site factors include:

- Sited on a plateau near the confluence of the Tiete and Tamanduate rivers.
- The city is 750 metres above sea level and separated from the coast by an escarpment called the Serra do Mar.
- The coastal location offered advantages for port development with associated industries such as warehousing, food processing, petrol chemicals and an integrated steelworks.
- Population increased due to natural factors such as high birth rates and decreasing death rates.
- Migration from rural areas due to **push factors** include: low incomes, lack of education, health facilities, employment and general low quality of living.
- This can be combined with **pull factors** such as possibility of industrial employment with improved income, better housing, education and health opportunities, family ties and an all round improvement in the quality of life. All of these factors helped to rapidly increase the city's population.

EUROPEAN REGIONAL INEQUALITIES

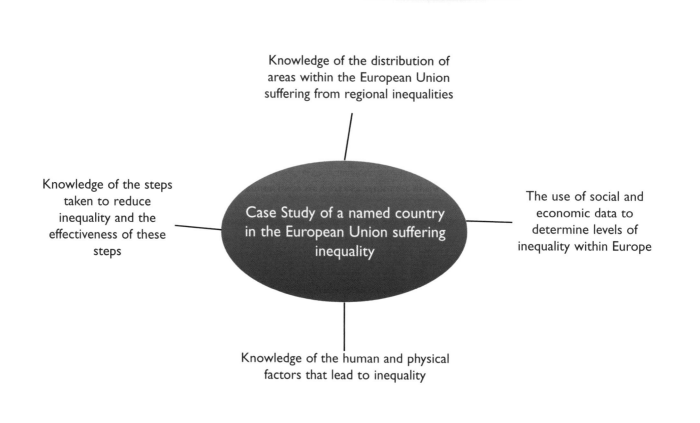

Knowledge of the distribution of areas within the European Union suffering from regional inequalities

Knowledge of the steps taken to reduce inequality and the effectiveness of these steps

Case Study of a named country in the European Union suffering inequality

The use of social and economic data to determine levels of inequality within Europe

Knowledge of the human and physical factors that lead to inequality

Referring to either the EU in general or specific case studies or named areas within the UK and individual EU countries which you have studied:

Key Point 1
You should be able to describe general socio-economic patterns shown on maps of the EU, e.g. 'Euro core and periphery' or on maps of individual countries within the EU.

Refer to Figure 5·1
Areas belonging to the Euro core include, for example, London and the south east (sometimes referred to as Roseland), Paris and the Ruhr / Rhine area. Refer to these areas by name, naming the more well-off areas as well as those which are apparently poorer according to the statistics given.

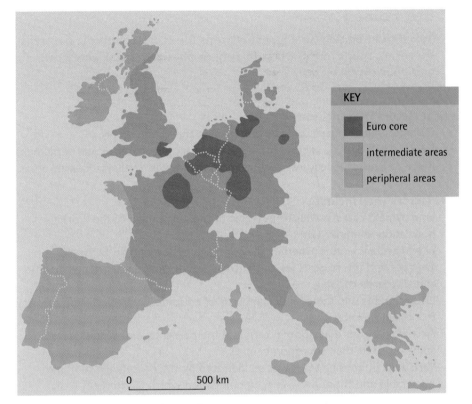

Figure 5·1 – Euro core and periphery

Key Point 2

You should be able to suggest the types of socio-economic indicators which can be used to produce such maps and comment on their usefulness

Indicators may include:
- Average income per head.
- The level of EU support per head of population.
- The level of private investment per head of population.
- The number of cars per head of population.
- The percentage of long term unemployed.
- The percentage employed in primary / secondary / tertiary industrial sectors; the percentage in higher education.
- These indicators, when used together are very useful in determing areas which are economically sound or areas which may have severe economic and social problems. Individual statistics such as GDP do not always reveal the true situation since they are highly generalised.
- Conclusions based on maps based on individual pieces of data should be treated with caution. Only when this data is combined with other statistics can a more realistic appraisal be made of the condition of certain areas or countries.

Key Point 3

You should be able to suggest reasons for socio-economic patterns shown on maps of the EU referring to physical, social, economic and political factors

Physical factors may include:
- Climate, which impacts on tourism, farming and water supply.
- Relief, which directly affects communications, farming patterns and settlement.
- Refer to landscape features such as mountain ranges / valleys / coastal areas.

Social factors may include:
- Employment rates, especially in terms of the percentage of the working population unemployed.
- Life expectancy rates, whether they are high or lower than European averages and the reasons for this such as health care, diets, average income and standards of living.
- Literacy rates and the overall standards of education provision from primary to college / university.
- Access to higher education in terms of the percentage of school leavers going on to further education centres.
- Variations in housing standards as indicated by the percentage of home ownership and those living in accommodation which fail to meet basic tolerable standards.

Economic factors may include:
- The level of industrialisation often indicated by industrial output and employment data.
- The availability of raw materials such as minerals.
- The quality of communication networks including road, rail and air.
- GDP or GNP figures as an indication of the area's wealth.
- The percentage of working population employed in industry and agriculture.
- A measure of industrial output in manufacturing industry.
- The occurrence of industrial problems such as overdependence on certain industries, e.g. declining traditional industries (coalmining/iron and steel), tourism.
- The continuing development of sunrise industries such as electronics.
- The level of government support to industrial areas in the form of loans, grants and subsidies.

Political factors may include:
- Government intervention within the economy, e.g. subsidising certain industries.
- National versus European legislation which can lead to complications in legal situations.
- Political instability which may involve continual change of governments and governing parties.

Key Point 4

You should be able to comment on the accuracy of given statements describing socio-economic patterns shown on maps of the EU

In your comments you may
Use table data to support your arguments as to the accuracy of given statements, referring, for example, to:
- employment data, such as percentage employed in different sectors of the economy (such as primary, secondary and service industries and agriculture)
- GDP and GNP figures
- migration rates, indicating industrial decline or growth in certain areas
- Compare and contrast areas which are economically developed or developing by referring to growth rates if given.

Key Point 5

You should be able to describe problems faced by peripheral EU areas, the steps taken to solve or alleviate these problems and make comments on the effectiveness of measures taken

Your answer will depend on the areas chosen but generally could refer to:

Economic problems:
- such as low investment in industry
- a high percentage of population employed in primary as opposed to the other better paid sectors of industry
- a poor infrastructure such as a poor maintained communications system
- long term poverty and low wages, e.g. often found in agricultural areas in Mediterranean Europe.

Social problems:
- high levels of unemployment, especially in manufacturing and teritiary industries
- increasing migration rates, especially increasing numbers of emigrants
- chronic crime rates associated with poverty levels
- deprivation, especially children suffering from malnutrition or poor living standards
- welfare dependency with many requiring considerable amounts of state aid
- depopulation and ageing populations caused by the emigration of those in the economically least-dependent age groups.

DEVELOPMENT & HEALTH

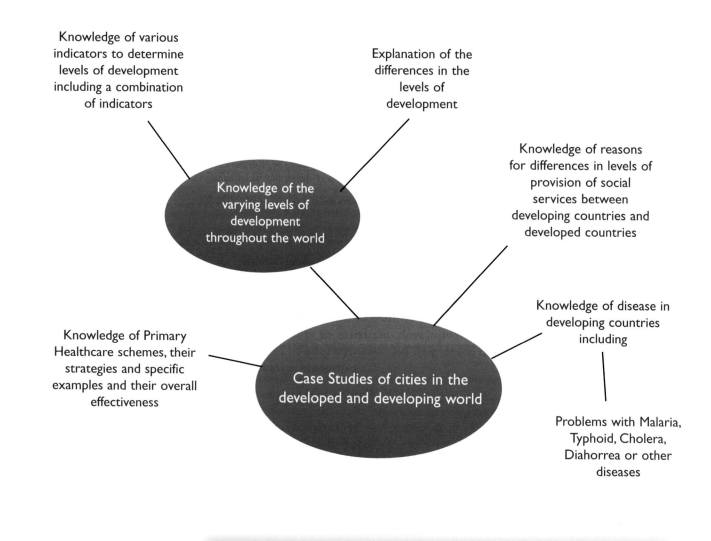

Knowledge of various indicators to determine levels of development including a combination of indicators

Explanation of the differences in the levels of development

Knowledge of reasons for differences in levels of provision of social services between developing countries and developed countries

Knowledge of the varying levels of development throughout the world

Knowledge of Primary Healthcare schemes, their strategies and specific examples and their overall effectiveness

Case Studies of cities in the developed and developing world

Knowledge of disease in developing countries including

Problems with Malaria, Typhoid, Cholera, Diahorrea or other diseases

Key Point 1

You should be able to identify economic and social indicators of development and show how these can illustrate different levels of development of countries

Economic indicators may include:
- Gross National Product (GNP) or Gross Domestic (GDP) Product statistics.
- Data relating to average income per capita.
- Data relating to the relative percentage of the workforce employed in industry and agriculture figures showing steel production tonnes / capita.
- Average electricity consumption kw / capita.
- Trade patterns in terms of Import and Export figures.
- Trade balances in terms of surplus or deficits.

Social indicators include:
- Birth rates / death rates / infant mortality rates / life expectancy rates.
- Population structure in terms of the distribution of age and sex.
- Average calorie intake per capita.
- The average number of people per doctor.
- literacy rates as an indication of the level of education.

Note that decisions on levels of development should be based on a number of indicators used together rather on individual indicators such as GNP.

The use of single indicators can be misleading since the data is based on averages and these do not reveal the whole situation.

For example, average per capita income or GDP per capita for Saudi Arabia may seem high and suggest a high level of development but income distribution is very unequal, varying from extremely high to very low.

Similarly GNP may indicate a high level but be based on a single commodity such as oil. Taken together to produce combined indices such the *'Physical Quality of Life Index'* (PQLI) or the *Human Development Index* (HDI), this gives a much more accurate picture of the stage of development of any given country.

Key Point 2

You should be able to identify different levels of development from given resources such as a table or map and be able to suggest suitable socio-economic indicators which could be used to produce maps showing, for example, economically developed and less developed countries

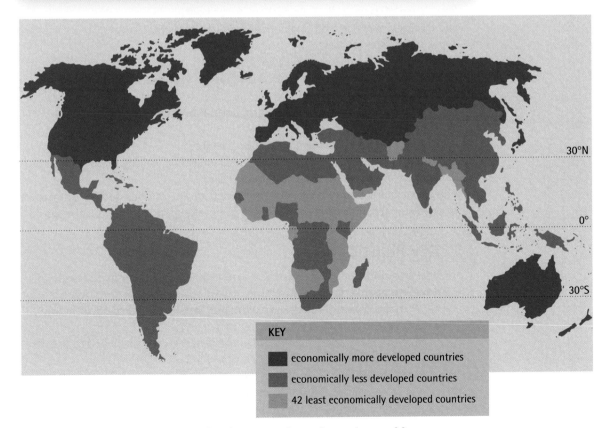

KEY

■ economically more developed countries

■ economically less developed countries

■ 42 least economically developed countries

Figure 6·1 – Levels of economic development throughout the world

Using the data outlined in Key Idea 1, maps can be drawn on the basis of indices to show the distribution of developed and developing countries (EMDCs and ELDCs).

Tables and diagrams based on this data can also depict countries at different stages of development.

Areas with low Gross National Product, high birth rates, low life expectancy rates, low literacy rates, low income per capita and a high percentage of the workforce working in agriculture would be best described as developing countries. The opposite situation would apply to developed countries.

Key Point 3

You should be able to describe and account for similarities and differences on such maps and be able to describe the kind of indicators which would be appropriate to use in the construction of measures of development, e.g. Human development index

Referring to case studies in developing countries

Description would relate to regions and countries which have common levels of development.

Explanation would refer to both physical and human factors such as:

- Climate factors such as rainfall reliability, which could affect the occurrence of droughts and floods.
- Resources such as industrial raw materials and agricultural output.
- Health standards in terms of the level of medical care available.
- Prevalence of various diseases such as water bourne diseases (cholera, typhoid) and diseases resulting from malnutrition and poor diets.
- Types of industry present.
- Types of imports and exports.
- Demographic trends such as birth, death and growth rates, infant mortality rates and average life expectancy.
- Food supply in terms of average calorie consumption per person and the availability of balance diets.
- Agricultural output in average yields per hectare.
- Variations in housing standards within cities indicating varying levels of wealth.
- Comments on presence of shanty town areas.
- The social and economic indicators discussed earlier can be used in combination to produce maps showing varying levels of development throughout the world.

Key Point 4

You should be able to describe and explain differences in levels of development and explain the limits of some indicators such as GNP in accurately reflecting different levels of standard of living within any one country

Reasons might include factors such as:
- Countries such as Saudi Arabia, United Arab Emirates and Brunei have prospered due to oil and gas reserves.
- Singapore, South Korea and Taiwan have encouraged the development of industry and commerce due to their entrepreneurial skills and have prospered.
- Countries such as Ethiopia or Chad lack natural resources and experience recurring droughts leading to famines.
- Some countries, e.g. Bangladesh suffer natural disasters such as floods / cyclones.
- Political instability, problems of rapid population growth and civil disorder also affect economic growth in many developing countries.

Accuracy of development indicators:
- As noted earlier, the use of one individual factor could be misleading, especially if that factor is based on average figures, e.g. income per capita or GNP.
- This does not reveal the possible wide variations existing within a country with some very wealthy people whilst others live at subsistence level within the same country.
- For example, in some Middle Eastern oil-producing countries GNP might appear to rank alongside those of highly developed countries but this wealth is not evenly spread across the population.
- Caution must also be used when looking at some indicators relating to social and economic development levels in, for example, Brazil or India.
- Using a combination of indicators to produce a quality of life index is the best method of assessing levels of development in any given country.

Key Point 5

You should know the factors which affect levels of malnutrition leading to a downward spiral of poverty and poor health

- Malnutrition results not only from a lack of food but the lack of the necessary vitamins, proteins and carbohydrates which contribute to a balanced and healthy diet.
- Diets which are based on one basic food source such as rice lack this variety supplied by nutritious foods.
- This happens in many countries throughout the world, notably south-east Asia and the Indian sub-continent.
- Consequently, a significant proportion of the population is unhealthy due to malnutrition and unable to resist even the most simple of diseases.
- Many people are debilitated and unable to work for any length of time.
- Industrial and agricultural output suffers and this eventually has a serious effect on the whole economy of countries in the developing world.
- Those suffering from malnutrition may not generate enough income for themselves and their families in order to pay for the basic necessities of life: food, accommodation, education and healthcare. Poverty ensues and, without any financial assistance from outside sources, it continues throughout the lifespan of those affected.

Key Point 6

You should be able to describe and explain differences in the provision of safe water and sanitation particularly between urban and rural areas

- Lack of clean, safe water leads to the contraction of many water-borne diseases such as typhoid, schistosomiasis, cholera, diahorrea.
- Lack of clean water may be due to physical factors such as drought or economic factors such as lack of funding for sanitation and water supply to households in poorer countries.
- These problems tend to occur more in poorer agricultural areas which rely on local water sources such as rivers and streams which can become contaminated.
- Urban areas usually have sanitation and water supplies although they may not be available to all residents, particularly those in squatter areas or shanty towns.

Key Point 7

You should be able to discuss the factors responsible for wide variations in life expectancy rates throughout the world

Life expectancy (or the average age people can expect to live to) depends on a wide variety of factors including:
- Diet, lifestyle, level of income, employment status, quality of living accommodation.
- Levels of pollution, prevalance of both contagious and infectious diseases.
- Levels of healthcare available, genetic factors.
- The influence of environmental factors such as climate, proximity to breeding grounds of disease carriers such as mosquitos.
- The occurrence of environmental hazards such as earthquakes, floods and droughts.
- People in developing countries tend to have significantly lower life expectancy rates than people living in developed countries.
- Life expectancy is closely related to levels of development which can vary greatly even within those countries termed developing world countries.

For any named infectious or water-related disease you have studied

Key Point 8

You should be able to describe the human and physical factors which contribute to the spread of the disease and describe the methods used to control the disease and comment on their success

Normally you are expected to be able to comment on one disease from a given list including for example malaria, schistomiasis and cholera.

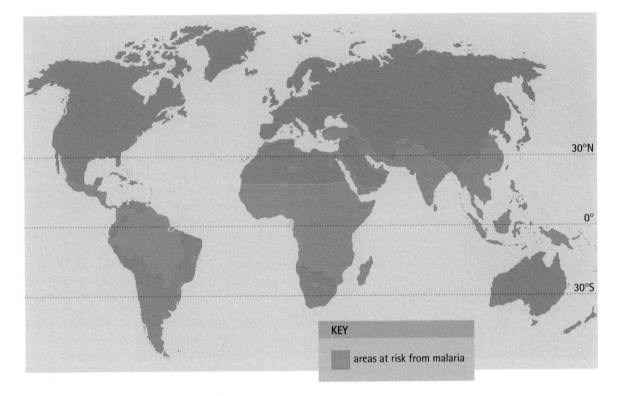

KEY

areas at risk from malaria

Figure 6·2 – Areas at risk from malaria

Malaria
- Malaria is basically spread by a vector which carries the disease parasite, namely the female anopheles mosquito.
- They pick up the disease by taking blood meals from infected persons; they then pass it on in the next blood meal through their saliva.
- These mosquitos breed in stagnant water (marshlands under certain climatic conditions) in generally hot, wet climates (a minimum temperature of 16°C).
- The disease can spread very rapidly throughout an area unless certain measures are taken to limit and control it.
- Mosquitoes have become resistant to many insecticides including DDT and malaria itself has adapted to resist certain drugs which were formerly used to cure it.
- As yet there is no vaccine available to prevent infection although great efforts are being made to produce one in medical research facilities.

Methods used to control the disease include:
- Drainage of areas with stagnant water, e.g. swamps and water management schemes to destroy breeeding grounds of mosquitoes near rivers.
- The use of insecticides such as malathion.
- The use of nets to protect people from mosquitoe bites while they are sleeping.
- The use of drugs to control the disease, e.g. quinine or derivatives of this drug – chloroquin. The use of village health centres and issue of information / education through primary healthcare schemes.
- Releasing water from dams to drown larvae.
- Using egg white sprayed on to stagnant surfaces to suffocate larvae.

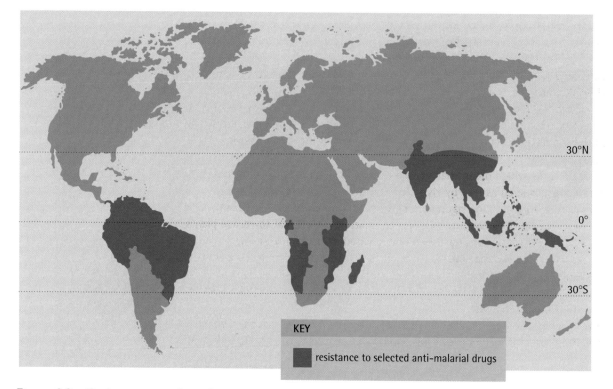

Figure 6·3 – Resistance to selected anti-malarial drugs

- The introduction of small fish in padi fields to eat larvae.
- The planting of eucalytus trees to absorb moisture.
- The application of mustard seeds into water areas which drag larvae below water surface and drown them.

Effectiveness of the methods:

- These measures have met with *varying degrees of success*.
- No effective vaccines have been produced although several test studies in China are achieving progress.
- Much depends on local population applying themselves to suggested precautions and taking medication regularly.
- Malaria remains a widespread debilitating and fatal disease in many parts of the developing world.

Referring to case studies from developing world countries (ELDCs)

Key Point 9

You should explain the impact of lack of clean water and poor sanitation on disease rates and efforts to tackle and improve provision of clean water and better sanitation

Depending on the country / countries you have studied you might refer to:

- Diseases such as cholera, typhoid and diahorrea is transmitted through bacteria carried in dirty water.
- Due to a lack of available clean water supplies many people are forced to cook and drink water from unclean sources such as streams.
- Lack of proper sanitation and sewage disposal plants mean that raw sewage can infect local water supplies resulting in increased incidence of disease infection, especially in shanty town areas with high concentrations of population.

Measures:

- Producing wells which mean that people do not have to draw water from unclean sources such as nearby rivers or streams.
- Having access to water management schemes to provide access to clean water.
- Improvements in the provision of in-house sanitation and local sewerage plants within cities and rural areas have been introduced in many developing countries.
- This has helped to reduce disease rates since disease bacteria which survives in raw sewage is destroyed.
- Most of these efforts are based on foreign aid schemes and charity donations through self-help schemes.
- Lack of money and ever increasing debt problems severely restrict the efforts of the governments of many developing countries in successfully tackling this problem.

Key Point 10

You should be able to discuss the reasons for high infant mortality rates and the efforts to reduce these high rates and their effectiveness

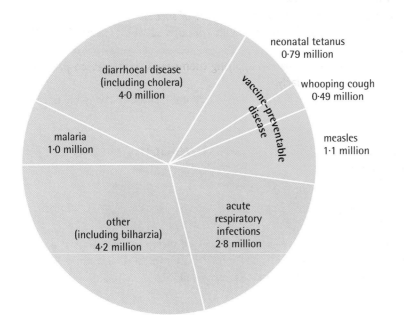

Figure 6·4 – Causes of deaths of children under 5 in the developing world

Reasons include:
- A lack of food causing starvation and malnutrition due to famine.
- A lack of proper medical care due to having few doctors and other trained medical staff.
- Poor medical provision including a limited supply of vaccinations and treatment for various diseases.
- A lack of clean water supplies and the transmission of many water-borne diseases such as cholera, schistosomiasis, malaria, typhoid and diahorrea resulting in infant deaths.
- Inedequate housing which may be very basic and have a serious lack of basic amenities such as cooking facilities, water and electricity supplies.
- A large part of the population living in shanty towns with poor access to even the most basic sanitary provision. This also badly affects the health of infants.

Efforts to reduce the problem include:
- Education programmes on the use of birth control which reduces the size of families giving children a better chance of survival.
- More effective hygene control being taught for example, using tablets to sterilise drinking water and boiling water to kill germs.
- Foreign aid programmes to provide food and medical supplies for children.
- Assistance from local government authorities to provide and encourage self-help schemes to improve living conditions for poverty stricken families.
- Governments are also investing in various programmes to help improve agricultural output The provision of additional medical facilities especially through primary healthcare schemes.

Key Point 11

You should know how primary healthcare methods are used to improve health standards and explain why they are appropriate. You should also explain how disease prevention can benefit developing world countries

Figure 6·5 – Summary of primary healthcare

Strategies of primary healthcare might include:

- The use of 'barefoot' doctors who are cheaper to train and therefore larger numbers can be used to service wider areas.
- Barefoot doctors are not doctors but local people trained in basic first-aid medical care. They can dispense medical care for minor ailments including giving injections when necessary.
- Through 'barefoot' doctors, a greater percentage of the population can be treated than if they had to rely on properly trained and qualified doctors.
- The use of oral rehydration treatment to tackle diarrhoea is cheap and easily admimistered. Costs are reduced by referring only the most serious and complex cases to hospitals.
- Routine medical situations are dealt with at local clinics.
- There are efforts to increase the development of a network of local clinics.
- There is the development of local health education programmes, especially in urban areas.
- More widespread use of cheaper pharmaceuticals rather than more expensive drugs which can be just as effective.
- Generally these measures have been regarded as very effective especially in reducing costs of medical care.
- Often these are supported by national policies, e.g. in India.
- Aid programmes which focus on primary healthcare are often more effective than any which provide large scale medical programmes such as the building of a large hospital which may treat only a limited minority of cases.

GLOSSARY OF ASSOCIATED TERMS

Appropriate technology: This involves the use of machinery and equipment which is best suited to the needs, skills and wealth of local communities.

Bilateral Aid: This is aid given from one country to another.

High technology: This is the use of advanced, sophisticated machinery which requires a high degree of skill to operate.

Intermediate technology: This is machinery and equipment which is of a higher level than basic primitive equipment but not as advanced as high technology.

Long-term aid: This is aid which is intended to be used over a long period of years to help a country to develop for example its industry, farming, transport system, education and health care systems.

Low technology: This is equipment which is very basic and cheap (ox drawn ploughs, wood burning ovens).

Multilateral aid: This is aid given from a group of countries through agencies such as United Nations to poorer coutries.

Official aid: This is either bilateral or multilateral aid given to a country.

Primary healthcare: This is a system designed to provide basic health and medical care to people in Economically less developed countries (ELDCs or developing countries) which is cost-effective and more readily available to people suffering from relatively minor health complaints. Rather than use highly trained medical staff or expensive hospitals, it relies on people who have basic medical skills and is therefore available to a larger number of the population.

Self-help schemes: These are projects in which local people become involved to improve their living conditions.

Short-term aid: This is aid given immediately to help an area recover from a major disaster such as a flood, drought, famine, or earthquake.

Tied aid: This is aid given but with conditions usually if the receiving country uses the money given to buy manufactured goods from the donor country.

United Nations Organisation: A world wide organisation of which nearly all of the world's countries are members. It has a wide range of functions such as world health, world finance, peacekeeping forces and various aid agencies.

Voluntary aid: This is aid given through charitable organisations such as Red Cross or Oxfam or Save the Children Fund.